"I love this book! Every so often a book c
flame that was started in my heart years ago when I was a young and
on-fire world changer. I love reading this type of book. I'm still a
fanatical, fiercely focused, imbalanced, apostolic type guy. I'm older
now, but more fervent than ever. If you're looking for an intelligent
and passionate book to stir you to dream big dreams of how
a movement can begin through your life and that will give you
practical tools to help implement those dreams, then read
Movements that Change the World!"

Floyd McClung
Founder/director of All Nations, South Africa. Author of *You See Bones, I See an Army:
Changing the Way We Do Church* and *Living on the Devil's Doorstep*.
www.floydandsally.org

"There are very few who have truly studied, dissected, and understood church multiplication movements at the core. My friend
Steve Addison has done his homework. I have anticipated this work
for some time and am pleased to report it is better than I ever
expected. Steve has put in the years of research and synthesizes his
vast amounts of experience, wisdom, and research into an easy-to-
read book."

Neil Cole
Founder of Church Multiplication Associates and Awakening Chapels.
Author of *Organic Church* and *Organic Leadership*.
www.cole-slaw.blogspot.com

"Steve has been tantalizing me with tales of this book for years.
He has talked to me about the content on numerous occasions.
The chapters are distilled from years of experience and thought,
and the final product has not disappointed. Practitioners and
thinkers with a passion for mission will want to read and re-read
this book."

Dr. Martin Robinson
Director of Together in Mission, UK. Co-author of *Metavista: Bible,
Church and Mission in an Age of Imagination*.
www.togetherinmission.org

"An important book for our times—well researched, well written, and well thought out. Steve identifies the essential qualities that have defined movements of the Spirit throughout the ages. The stories he tells—biblical, historical, contemporary, and personal—give us hope for fresh movements of God in our day."

Dr. Robert E. Logan
CoachNet International Ministries. Author of *Be Fruitful and Multiply.*
www.coachnet.org

"As I read through your manuscript I felt that I had met a long-lost brother. I had to read it through in a single sitting because it pulled me through from start to finish. Excellent work, brother! This will be a valuable contribution to our growing understanding of church planting movements and their history, scope, and nature. I love the way you have woven together insights from sociology, history, Scripture, contemporary case studies, and even personal experience. I will be recommending this to everyone I know. Thank you for vividly reminding us that Jesus did not found a religion, but a movement!"

David Garrison
International Mission Board, Southern Baptist Convention.
Author of *Church Planting Movements: How God is Redeeming a Lost World.*
www.churchplantingmovements.com

" 'Adaptive, innovative, and consuming.' Those words characterize the movements Steve Addison describes and prescribes in his book. They also depict the book—pick it up and it won't let go of you. I couldn't put it down till it finished re-arranging my mind. This is a keeper!"

Ralph Moore
Founding pastor of Hope Chapel Kaneohe Bay, Hawaii.
Author of *How To Multiply Your Church.*
www.ralphmoorehawaii.com

"In this book Steve Addison demonstrates the desire of God from the biblical era until today. He casts a compelling future vision by tracing God's discernible lessons demonstrated in movements. Steve taps into the heart hunger of the growing number of us that want to see God do something great. Your heart will be stirred while you read *Movements that Change the World*. If you are like me, you will be prompted to stop and pray, 'Lord, do it again, for the sake of our communities and nations—for every man, woman, and child!'"

Ed Stetzer

Missiologist. Author of *Planting Missional Churches*.
www.edstetzer.com

movements

that change the world

Steve Addison

MISSIONAL PRESS

Published by Missional Press
149 Golden Plover Drive
Smyrna, DE 19977
www.missional-press.com

Printed in the United States of America.

ISBN: 10: 0-9798053-7-6
ISBN: 13: 978-0-9798053-7-0

Cover concept and design by peterbergmeier.com

To Michelle

These men have caused trouble all over the world.

Acts 17:6

Acknowledgements

It was about twenty years ago that I became fascinated with movements and discovered my calling was to fuel church planting movements. It has been a long, hard road to get to the place of readiness to write this book—hard, but good. God is faithful, and along the way he has brought so many people into my life that have helped me go the distance.

To Peter Costello, Bill Hallam, Pete Fitzgerald, Nigel Barr, Rod Denton, Terry Walling, Rick Paynter, Bob Logan, Sam Metcalf, Andrew Herbert, Alan Hirsch, Craig Winkler, and Buck Rogers— thank you. Thanks also to Patrick Innes and Rod Smith who walked with me through the dark days of 2007.

Thanks also to Val Gresham, my writing coach and editor; to David Phillips of Missional Press who saw the potential of this project; and to Alister Cameron, my blogologist.

Dad, thanks for your example of Christian leadership and, even more, for your commitment to Mum right to the end.

Michelle, you are my one and only love. You stood by me and never stopped believing in God's call on my life. Thank you.

Contents

Foreword - Alan Hirsch

Steve and I go a long way back. We shared many of the same classes in seminary. It soon became clear that we also shared a passion for the idea of movements and their relevance for mission today. As we met over the years, we have shared many ideas that we think are vital to recover in our day if we are going to reverse the decline of the Church at the dawn of the 21st Century. The result has been one of the most theologically fertile friendships that I have ever had. We argued some, agreed mostly, and refined our thinking all the time, but definitely we mutually enriched each other's views on this vital topic over the last twenty years. Steve's friendship has been a kind of mentorship that has left me a much richer person, for which I am profoundly thankful. His influence can be found throughout my own writings on this topic.

Steve brings a passionate love for God and his people to the task of writing. In *Movements that Change the World* you will discover an engaging description of the dynamics of missionary movements and how to initiate, maintain, and extend them. Behind this unencumbered, non-technical portrayal of the examples of history and their ongoing witness lies a lifetime of research that brings together disparate insights from theology, church history, sociology, business studies, missiology, leadership studies, spirituality, and everything in between. This book is a labor of love that has taken decades of service to prepare.

Instructed by the lessons of history, fueled by a missionary's vision of what the world can be, and guided by deep commitment to orthodox, historic Christianity, this book should be read by all who wish to rediscover what it means for Christianity to be a missional movement again in the West.

Alan Hirsch
Founder/director of Forge Mission Training Network and Shapevine.com.
Author of *The Forgotten Ways* and co-author of *The Shaping of Things to Come*.
www.theforgottenways.org

Foreword - Bob Roberts Jr.

I had the privilege of meeting Steve for the first time in 2008 at a small global gathering of influential pastors who had all planted churches and were planting churches out of their churches. I've followed Steve's blog and writings for years, and I'm delighted he has gathered his insights into book form. Studying church planting movements is challenging because of all the history, facts, and contexts – it isn't easy work, and sometimes it is not easy work to read! That's where Steve comes in!

Steve has done his homework and has all the academic qualifications necessary to identify the five core characteristics of a church planting movement—maybe any movement. The good news is he does this in a way that enables all of us, not just the academics, to understand it. After all, it's going to be our "everyday disciples" that will make this happen. He then gives both historical and contemporary examples to illustrate how it works.

The character and experiences of the book's author are huge in terms of how much can you trust what's written. That is another point where Steve really stands out. He lives this stuff. He has planted churches, been involved and is recognized as one of the top global leaders in training church planters, and is also a student and researcher of church planting and movements.

I not only endorse this book but also will require all of our interns, students, and residents to read it. Thanks, Steve, for a great gift to the body of Christ!

Bob Roberts Jr.
Lead pastor of NorthWood Church in Keller, Texas.
Author of *The Multiplying Church* and *Glocalization*.
www.glocal.net

Patrick

I, Patrick, a sinner, unlearned, resident in Ireland, declare myself to be a bishop. Most assuredly I believe that what I am I have received from God. And so I live among barbarians, a stranger and exile for the love of God. He is witness that this is so.[1]

Letter to Coroticus

Can anything good come out of Ireland?

When Alaric and his army of Visigoths marched into Rome to loot and plunder in 410 AD, it was as though the world had ended.[2] It had been eight hundred years since an enemy last breached Rome's defenses. Rome, the Eternal City, was the heart and soul of the greatest empire in history.

The sack of Rome sent a shock wave throughout the Empire. Yet it was hardly noticed on the fringes of the Empire, except perhaps by the Irish pirates who for years had been taking advantage of the withdrawal of the Roman navy to attack the west coast of Britain.

Patrick was sixteen years old when the Irish raiders stormed his village in Roman Britain.[3] Until that day he had lived a privileged life. He was born into the British land-owning aristocracy. His grandfather was a priest, and his father was a magistrate and church leader. The life of a Roman magistrate was one of honor and privilege. The position was hereditary; one day Patrick would rule as part of Roman nobility in Britain. The raiders seized him, along with servants from his father's estate, and returned across the sea to the pagan land of Ireland where they sold him into slavery. The year was 405 AD.

For the next six years Patrick lived the lonely and hard life of a slave, working as a shepherd. Isolation, hunger, and cold brought him misery, and misery taught him humility. God worked powerfully in Patrick's suffering to remake him from the inside out. He freed Patrick from dependence on wealth and his place in society. God rescued Patrick from himself and made his heart captive to the love of Christ.

According to Patrick, before his abduction he did not believe in the living God. As a slave, Patrick came to see the hand of God in his troubles. God broke through his defenses, and Patrick faced his unbelief and pride. Later he described how he turned to God who he realized had been watching over him all the time. He became aware of God's protection, and he discovered that God loved him as a father loves his son.

Outwardly nothing changed for Patrick; he was still a captive in a harsh foreign land, but he saw life differently. The land of his captivity had become the land of his freedom in God. The slave of men had become a son of God.

The love and fear of God grew in him. Patrick recalled how he learned to pray continually as he worked. At night he stayed out in the forests and on the mountains to pray. He would rise before dawn to pray in the icy coldness of the Irish winter. This was no burden to him but a delight because the Spirit was burning in him.

One night God spoke to him in a dream and revealed that there was a ship waiting to take him home. There was one problem— two hundred miles of dangerous territory lay between him and the coast. Patrick made his escape and began the long journey home as a runaway slave.

The details are sketchy, but he reached the ship and eventually made it back to his family and resumed the life he once had in

Britain. Perhaps he looked forward to inheriting his father's position in society and all the privileges that went with it. But God, who is the initiator in this story, had other plans for Patrick.

Patrick woke one night to the voices of the people he had known in Ireland crying out, "We beg you, come and walk with us again!" Their cry pierced his heart. God was calling him to return—and he did.

In time he was ordained as a priest and bishop despite his limited education and experience. Later Patrick faced opposition to his authority from church leaders, but he believed that it was God who had appointed him, an uneducated sinner, to be a missionary bishop to the Irish.

When Patrick returned to Ireland, it had been four hundred years since Christ commanded his disciples to go to the nations, yet the gospel was largely contained within the borders of the Roman Empire.[4] God took the initiative to transform a teenager with an inherited faith into an apostle compelled by the Spirit to take the gospel to the ends of the earth. The shepherd-boy slave had become the slave of Christ and apostle to Ireland.

Patrick's troubles had prepared him well for his mission. Through them he had become devoted to Christ and the gospel. His heart longed to reach the "barbarians" beyond the borders of civilization. His lack of formal training contributed to his openness to new and effective methods.

In contrast, the church of the Roman Empire was not interested in taking the gospel beyond the borders of Greco-Roman civilization. Romans regarded the tribes outside the Empire, such as the Celts, the Goths, and the Huns, as barbarians. The religious world of the Irish Celts was inhabited by a bewildering array of gods, goddesses, and spirits of the sky, earth, and water; the Celts also believed in the magical powers of ancestors and divine animals.[5] For the church of the Roman Empire, these pagan barbarians were beyond the missionary concern of God.

Patrick, however, saw the need and opportunity to reach these

Irish barbarians. He traveled throughout Ireland to remote and dangerous places to preach, baptize converts, and ordain clergy for the new churches. From nobles to slaves, the Irish were ready to hear and obey the gospel. Thousands of them responded to Patrick's preaching and turned from their pagan idols to serve the living God. Many of the converts took up Patrick's challenge to join his missionary band.

Patrick gave the Irish the gift of non-Roman Christianity. Since the conversion of Emperor Constantine in 312 AD, Christianity had been closely identified with Roman culture and power. Yet Patrick liberated Ireland without the backing of imperial power. Instead he lived and communicated the gospel in ways that connected and resonated deeply with Irish hopes and concerns. He taught the Irish that they could become followers of Christ without having to become like Romans.

Steadily the gospel worked its power through the Irish tribal society. Patrick embraced the best of Celtic culture and redeemed it to serve the gospel. He fought those aspects of Irish culture that did not conform to the gospel. He ended the slave trade, and under the gospel's influence, murder and tribal warfare decreased. In place of a warrior society, Patrick provided a living alternative. He showed the Irish that it was possible to be brave—to expect every day to be murdered, betrayed, enslaved—and yet to be a man of peace with no fear of death because of the promises of an almighty God.[6]

Patrick faced fierce opposition. He had to contend with the magic of the Druids (the powerful priestly caste of Celtic society), and he faced the violence of local chieftains. On one occasion, newly baptized Christians were attacked by British raiders from the west coast of Patrick's homeland. The men were slaughtered, and the women and children were kidnapped, some of them still wearing their baptismal robes.

Just as distressing was the opposition from other church leaders. Patrick's writings make it clear that influential sections of the church disapproved of him, despite his role in the conversion of much of Ireland.[7] Patrick's worst critics were the bishops in Britain. They were not interested in taking the gospel to the Irish. They may have initially tolerated the appointment of such a poorly educated novice, but as the Christian faith spread throughout Ireland some church leaders questioned whether Patrick was the right person to lead such a successful and potentially lucrative ministry.[8]

Patrick was deeply conscious that his authority to preach the gospel came from God, but he was also painfully aware of his limitations and of his many critics. He was embarrassed by his lack of formal theological training and the poor quality of his Latin. His writings do not reveal the training of scholar, but they do reveal the heart of a man compelled by the love of Christ, led by the Spirit, and guided by the Scriptures.[9]

Patrick made church structures serve his mission to Ireland. The church of the Roman Empire was based around the cities where the local bishop was supreme. The Irish were a rural and tribal people. Unlike the civilized Romans, they had no settled towns, roads, currency, written law, government bureaucracy, or taxation. Irish society was decentralized and organized around tribes led by local "kings."[10] So Patrick decentralized the church.

The Roman system was based on the diocese and the bishop. The life of the Celtic church revolved around the monastery, which was led by an abbot. The abbots selected the bishops, and the bishops were dependent on them.

Patrick's mobile missionary bands closely followed the example of Jesus and Paul, but the Roman church leaders did not approve. Patrick responded to his critics through his writings as best he could with his limited literary skills, but he did not let them stop him. Not only was his ministry at stake, but also the missionary movement that was about to be unleashed throughout Britain and Europe.

The Celtic missionary movement was not a highly organized or centrally controlled operation. Under Patrick's influence, wave after wave of Irish youth flooded into monastic life. Most monasteries began in remote places when their founders withdrew from the world only to be pursued by throngs of young men who were eager to follow their example.[11] Monastic founders responded to the call of Christ and gathered workers around them. Each founder developed his own Rule for his followers.[12]

The monasteries were places of spiritual devotion and learning, but they were also sending centers. The Irish church took on the character of a missionary movement. For centuries Ireland became a base from which Christianity spread throughout the British Isles and to much of western and northern Europe as monks followed the call to "go pilgrimage for Christ."[13]

Patrick's followers shared a love for classical literature and the pagan poets, but the Scriptures had first place in their hearts and minds.[14] They read them with passion rather than detached academic interest. Although few were great theologians, they were known for their spiritual authority and missionary zeal. Young men who once would have given their lives in feuds between the clans now gave their lives to plant the gospel wherever Christ led them.

Under the abbot, each missionary outpost made decisions in adapting to local needs and opportunities. They recruited new missionaries from the local people and sent them out to found new monasteries.[15] This made Celtic monasticism highly flexible, adaptable, and transplantable—everything that the church of the Roman Empire was not.

Ireland had no cities. The monasteries grew rapidly and became the first population centers; they were hubs of unprecedented prosperity, art, and learning.[16] A distinct Celtic Christian culture emerged. For hundreds of years missionaries and scholars went out from Ireland, while students from many lands came to Ireland and left inspired to become missionaries. These missionary monks founded the monasteries throughout Europe that would one day become great cities.[17]

Patrick's personal achievements were impressive, but his greater legacy was the missionary movement he inspired. The monasteries of the Celtic missionary movement became dynamic centers of spiritual devotion, learning, industry, and evangelism in a chaotic world.

The Irish monk Columba (521-597), whose grandfather had been baptized by Patrick, continued to shape the Celtic missionary movement. He and twelve companions left Ireland for the island of Iona off the coast of Scotland. Columba shared Patrick's commitment to the Bible and love for Christ; these inspired him with the same missionary zeal. At Iona he established a missionary base for the evangelization of the pagan Scots and Picts. Columba trained and sent out missionary monks who established a network of monasteries. For centuries Iona served as a center for training and sending out missionaries and the establishment of other sending centers throughout Ireland, Scotland, and northern England.

As the number of monasteries multiplied throughout Ireland, Britain, and the European continent, converts were won and new missionaries left to "go pilgrimage for Christ" wherever they felt his leading.

What part did the Roman church play in this story? Rome was the center of civil and ecclesiastical power. The Roman church had a distinguished history stretching back to the apostles. It had built efficient organizational systems throughout the empire, and it had money and clout. Yet the Roman church was strangely absent from the frontline of missionary expansion.

As the Roman Empire and civilization collapsed, it was not the Roman church but the church of the barbarian Celts that led the way in missionary endeavor and cultural transformation. The Celts had biblical simplicity and devotion to Christ on their side. They shaped their church structures and methods to fit their culture and missionary purpose. Rome had the resources, but the followers of Patrick had the zeal.

Patrick died in 461. As the western part of the Roman Empire crumbled and darkness spread over much of Europe, the light of the gospel shone brightly from remote Ireland. For the next five hundred years, the youth of Ireland and their disciples fanned out across Europe, winning converts, making disciples, and multiplying missionary outposts. Wherever they went they carried their books and their love of learning. They revitalized European culture and possibly saved civilization following the fall of the Roman Empire.

Characteristics of a missionary movement

God takes the initiative and chooses unlikely people, far from the center of ecclesiastical power. He works to remake them from the inside out. He inspires innovative insights regarding his mission and how it is to be carried out. Biblical truths and practices are rediscovered. A growing band of ordinary people emerges who have a heartfelt faith and missionary zeal that knows no bounds. Despite opposition from powerful forces within society and the existing church, the gospel spreads into unreached fields. The existing church is renewed, and society is transformed. Eventually every movement declines as it discovers that its treasure is buried in this world rather than the next. Meanwhile God goes looking for another lonely shepherd boy who is cold, hungry, and a long way from home.

The life-cycle pattern of new life, growth, maturity, and decline is a recurring theme of history. This book deals with the characteristics of missionary movements in their most dynamic expression. From Patrick's story we can identify five key characteristics of movements that change the world.

1.   White-hot faith

This story of a great missionary movement began with a teenage boy who was broken, lonely, and defeated. He lost his home, his family, and his position in society. He had lost everything, but he found the love of God in Christ and a call to preach the gospel.

Movements that change the world may eventually come to possess resources, learning, and power, but they do not begin with these things. Missionary movements begin with men and women who encounter the living God and surrender in loving obedience to his call.

2.   Commitment to a cause

Nothing was more important to Patrick and his followers than their faith in Christ and his cause. They expected a high degree of commitment from themselves and from one another. They attracted the youth of Ireland who gladly devoted their lives to the spread of the gospel. Their "otherworldly" faith paradoxically enabled them to be fearless and uncompromising agents of transformation in this world.

3.   Contagious relationships

When movements spread rapidly, they do so through preexisting networks of relationships. Patrick did not just win isolated individuals. His strategy was to reach whole clans with the gospel. Patrick removed unnecessary barriers to the spread of the gospel and the growth of the movement. The Scriptures were supreme, yet the monks had a love for both classical literature and the pagan poets. His missionary movement was at home in the existing culture and yet radically distinct from it. A truly Celtic church missionary movement emerged.

4.   Rapid mobilization

Patrick grew leaders from the people he reached. His missionaries did the same. There was a constant supply of workers moving throughout and beyond Ireland for centuries. They won new converts and recruited fresh workers wherever they traveled. None of this was centrally planned, funded, or controlled. There was the expectation that the same Spirit who had inspired Patrick would inspire others to follow his example. These workers were not known for their polished Latin or abstract theology. They were known for their missionary zeal and devotion to Christ.

5. Adaptive methods

Patrick structured the Celtic church for the spread of the gospel. The missionary order was at the head of church life. Celtic monasticism was supremely adaptable, flexible, and transferable in contrast to the static, rigid, and anchored nature of the Roman church. Patrick communicated the gospel in ways that affirmed the best of Celtic culture, ensuring that the Irish could follow Christ without having to become Romans. The heart of the gospel remained the same. The forms changed to fit the context and to serve the needs of an expanding movement while the unchanging gospel remained at the center of the movement.

Whenever and wherever we find dynamic missionary movements, we will find each of these characteristics in some form. Before we go on to look at each one in depth, we need first to understand what movements are and why they are important.

Introduction:
Why movements matter

Let me tell you why movements matter to me. I walked away from my faith in my late teens and early twenties. It didn't take long for my life to unravel. I wasn't happy with God, and I wasn't happy without him. I didn't think living as a Christian was possible. Then along came an Australian guy called Bill Hallam. He'd come to know Christ on the hippie trail between Amsterdam and Delhi through a ministry called Dilaram founded by Floyd and Sally McClung.[1]

I was impressed with Bill. There were times when I wanted to throw him out of my house because of the hard things he had to say, but I knew he loved me and I knew that Christ had changed his life. I hoped my life could change too.

I gave up running from God. Six months later I'd saved enough money to travel from Australia to Holland and join Dilaram. It was the late 1970s. I ended up on the "Ark" in Amsterdam. The Ark was Dilaram's discipleship community located on two large houseboats on a canal behind the central railway station.

There I learned how to experience the love of God in prayer and worship. I learned how to communicate the gospel to travelers from all over the world. I saw broken lives restored by the power of the Word and the Spirit in the context of a discipleship community.

There was Jean Claude, a deserter from the French Foreign

Legion who had come to faith. I was there the day Interpol came to arrest him. I shared a room with two former members of the Irish Republican Army, both new Christians. One eventually turned himself in and went to prison. I remember Dave, a six-foot-five-inch Scotsman and "rage-aholic," waving a hammer in front of my face and threatening to kill me. There were people with backgrounds in homosexuality, prostitution, Eastern religions, and drugs. Every year around forty of them came to faith and began the journey of discipleship.

I didn't know it at the time, but Dilaram was a movement. It began when God called the McClungs. Floyd was in India with Youth With A Mission when he passed a beggar on the street and realized the beggar was a young Westerner who had fallen on hard times. There were thousands of hippies on the road from London to Delhi. Many were searching for truth but instead got dysentery, hepatitis, and addicted to drugs.

Floyd and Sally set up the first Dilaram House in Kabul, Afghanistan. They took in ill and drug-dependent hippies, nursed them, talked to them about Jesus, and saw many come to know him. Soon Dilaram Houses were established in London, Amsterdam, Kathmandu, and Delhi. Many of the workers for these houses had come to faith through Dilaram.

I never forgot the lessons I learned through my time with Dilaram; I discovered the love of God, the call to discipleship, the power of the gospel to change lives, the work of the Holy Spirit, the importance of prayer and Christian community, and God's heart for the nations. These lessons became part of me and have guided me ever since. I also didn't mind meeting Michelle, the Australian girl I would eventually marry, in Amsterdam.

God uses missionary movements like Dilaram to remake people and to make history. That's why they are important to me.

What I would like to do is help you understand the dynamics of missionary movements by telling the stories and reflecting on the lessons they can teach us. I'd like to help you get in touch with the dreams God has given you to make a difference in the lives of lost people living in a broken world. I believe God can use these stories from history, from our contemporaries, and from around the world, to encourage our hearts, strengthen our resolve, and teach us about how he works through his people.

If you want to be a disciple of Jesus and if you want to make disciples, this book is for you.

Movements that change the world

Before we move on we should clarify what a movement is. In a general sense, movements are informal groupings of people and organizations pursuing a common cause. They are people with an agenda for change. Movements don't have members, but they do have participants. The goals of a movement can be furthered by organizations, but organizations are not the totality of a movement. A movement can have leading figures, but no one person or group controls a movement. Movements are made up of people committed to a common cause.

Think of the environmental movement. Where are its head-quarters? Where is the organization or leader who controls this movement? The reality is the environmental movement is composed of an array of interconnected leading figures, organizations, and participants. They may not all agree on the precise nature of their goals and methods, but they share a common cause.

For good or for evil, movements make history. So much of history is the result of the clash of movements vying over their conflicting visions of how the world should be.

Religious, cultural, and political movements shaped the last century. Wars were waged over nationalism, communism, and Islamic fundamentalism. The civil rights movement, feminism, environmentalism, and the gay rights movement set the social agenda. A well-kept secret is that Pentecostalism, broadly defined, was the largest and most expansive movement of the last century.

Movements are characterized by discontent, vision, and action. Discontent unfreezes people from their commitment to the way things are. Movements emerge when people feel something needs to change. If the vacuum created by discontent is filled with a vision of a different future and action to bring change, then a movement is born.

Movements change people, and changed people change the world.

What Jesus started

Jesus was the first missionary. He didn't start an organization, he didn't write a book, and he didn't run for office. What Jesus did was to found a missionary movement that would one day span the globe.

Jesus began his life and ministry far from the center of power. He was a carpenter's son with a basic education. He was not formally trained as a rabbi. He was without social status and wealth. What mattered to Jesus was his relationship with his Father. He spent long hours in prayer. The Hebrew Scriptures permeated his life and his teaching. He won his victory over Satan by surrendering to the Father as an obedient Son.

Jesus went from town to town demonstrating the compassion and power of God as he healed the sick and cast out demons. He was drawn to ordinary people who knew they needed God: fishermen, tax collectors, farmers, prostitutes, soldiers, beggars, and notorious sinners. His mission was to seek and to save them by giving his life as a ransom for them.

Jesus bypassed the religious and community leaders and called ordinary people to join his missionary band. He called them to be with him, and he promised to teach them how to catch people. He taught them as they traveled together by foot and by boat. He taught them as he ministered to thousands and as he ministered to individuals.

Jesus spoke to crowds in the open air. He told stories to groups over a meal. He talked to individuals alone. He communicated with power and with simplicity, trusting the Father for the outcome.

When Jesus' disciples had learned just enough to be dangerous, he sent them out with empty pockets to preach, heal, and cast out demons.

Jesus contended fearlessly with his opponents and never gave ground. He called his hearers to turn from their sin and to turn to God for mercy and forgiveness. He set his face to go to Jerusalem and die a shameful criminal's death. He entrusted his life and the fruit of his ministry to God.

God the Father raised Jesus from the dead, defeating sin and death and Satan. Just when Jesus' disciples thought the job was done and it was time to put their feet up, Jesus commanded them to go and make disciples of every nation. He did not offer them resources or a plan. He just commanded them to go and promised his presence through the Holy Spirit.

That's how the mission of Jesus became a missionary movement.

The church Jesus founded was a missionary church. Its existence and activities were an expression of its missionary calling.[2] Its members were fearlessly determined to win others to faith in Jesus as the crucified and risen Messiah. Their mission field began at home in Jerusalem and Judea, and it extended to the ends of the earth. The goal and purpose of their missionary work was the making of disciples and the creation of communities of disciples. Disciples were people who turned from their old way of life, put their trust in Jesus, and obeyed his teaching.[3]

There is no other foundation for our mission than the good news of Christ crucified for our sins. Paul says the message of the cross is offensive to sinful humanity. It was offensive to Paul until he met Jesus on the Damascus road. Our mission is to proclaim the good news about Jesus in words and deeds by the power of the Holy Spirit.

The New Testament is a missionary document.[4] The Gospels tell the story of what Jesus *began* to do and teach, and Acts is about what Jesus continued to do through the Holy Spirit (Acts 1:1). In Acts people were converted and gathered into new churches. The New Testament epistles were written by missionaries concerned with the spiritual growth of Jesus' followers in community and in mission. If the early church had not been a missionary church—sharing the gospel of Jesus and making disciples—there would have been no church.

Our English words "mission," "missionary," and "missional" come from the Latin *missio*, meaning "the act of sending." *Missio* is the equivalent of the New Testament Greek word "apostle" from *apostolos*, meaning "one who is sent." Jesus told his disciples, "As the Father has *sent* me, I am *sending* you." Then he breathed on them and said, "Receive the Holy Spirit" (John 20:21b-22). The church as a missionary or missional movement is sent to carry on the ministry of Jesus in the power of the Spirit. Alan Hirsch reminds us that, "The mission of God flows directly through every believer and every community of faith that adheres to Jesus."[5] The church, in its very essence, is a missionary / missional movement with a mandate to take the good news of Jesus to world.

Today there appears to be some confusion over the terms "missionary" and "missional" when used as descriptors of the church. The words are identical in meaning. They refer to being sent by God into world. Unfortunately, when we hear the word "missionary" we tend to think of cross-cultural or overseas mission. When we hear the word "missional" the focus tends to be on mission in a first-world postmodern context. The mission of God knows no such cultural or geographic boundaries. There is only one missionary / missional mandate. There is only one missionary / missional church. There is only one missionary / missional movement that Jesus founded.

Mission has a threefold reality.[6] First, there is a message: mission assumes a distinct view of truth concerning the nature of God and the nature of salvation. Second, mission involves the communication of both truth and a new way of life. Third, the purpose of mission is conversion. People accept the message, are integrated into the community of faith, and begin to practice a new way of life—a new life committed to following Jesus and sharing the truth about him with others.

As a missionary movement, our message centers on Jesus Christ, the Son of God, who was crucified for our sin and is the only source of salvation for a lost world.

Second, as a missionary movement we have an agenda for change. Jesus calls all who would follow him to a new life of obedience to his will.

Third, mission involves the conversion of individuals and their inclusion into the body of Christ, which is the church, the people of God. There is no mission without the church, and there is no discipleship without the community of faith.

If this is what it means to be the missionary people of God, what do "missionaries" do? Eckhard Schnabel explains, "Missionaries establish contact with non-Christians, they proclaim the news of Jesus the Messiah and Savior (proclamation, preaching, teaching, instruction), they lead people to faith in Jesus Christ (conversion, baptism), and they integrate the new believers into the local community of the followers of Jesus (Lord's Supper, transformation of social and moral behavior, charity)."[7]

We have the message of the cross. We have new life in Christ. We have a mandate to make disciples and multiply churches—everywhere. We are a missionary people.

Why we're not all the same

I was corrupted in my first year of theological college. I discovered that church history is not just the history of ideas and events, it is also the history of movements. The church through history is in a constant state of upheaval and change, decline and resurgence.

Christianity is a movement of movements—monasticism, evangelicalism, and Pentecostalism, to name a few. These movements can find expression in movement organizations such as mission agencies and denominations. Movements are one of the key means by which God brings renewal and expansion to the church in its mission.

Each new movement has a unique contribution to make to the kingdom—its "founding charism" or gift of grace.[8] Monasticism modeled a deep devotion to Christ in the face of growing nominalism in the church. The Franciscans' gift to the church and the world was God's heart for the poor. The Reformation upheld the authority of Scripture and restored the truth of salvation by grace through faith. The Anabaptists emphasized the importance of discipleship and the believers' church. The Moravians were an inspiration as the first Protestant missionary order. The Methodists and Salvation Army combined evangelistic zeal and holiness with a heart for the poor. The Pentecostals rediscovered the untamed power of the Holy Spirit.

Where would we be today without the influence of these movements? What would we be left with today if their contributions were erased from history? They all had their shortcomings, yet God was at work through them, renewing his church in faithfulness to Christ and his cause.

The great church historian Kenneth Scott Latourette argued that one of the indications of the vitality of the Christian faith is the emergence of new movements. The periods of the greatest vigor and expansion of the Christian faith are the periods in which new movements arise.[9] The Christian movement is like a garden. A healthy garden is an ecosystem filled with diversity where new plants are always coming into existence, other plants are flourishing, and still others are dying and decaying. The garden lives on in a continuing state of renewal. It is through the birth and growth of new movements of churches and mission entities that God has renewed the Christian movement down through the ages.

In the renewal and expansion of the church, the breakthroughs *always* occur on the fringe of ecclesiastical power—*never* at the center.[10] In every generation, in some obscure place, God is beginning something new. That's where we need to be.

Is this book for you?

If you're a follower of Jesus, you don't have to start a missionary movement. You're already in one. This book is about helping you to understand what this means and how to participate in what God is already doing.

When I wrote this book, I had some people in mind. I thought of Mark and Fiona who have seen eighteen people come to know Christ over the last year and are wondering if these people are the beginning of a church plant.

I thought of Oscar, a pastor in Kenya who has grown a church from a dozen people to thousands. Even more important, the leaders he has grown are now planting churches in the suburbs and the slums of Nairobi, and that's just the beginning.

I thought of "Pauline" in China, a young woman in her twenties who is winning her friends to Christ and baptizing them secretly in a bathtub. She has a vision to multiply small house fellowships in her city.

I thought of Wayne and his team, who go visiting door to door in their impoverished community every week, caring for the sick, praying for people in need, helping out in practical ways, and sharing the good news of Jesus. Wayne is wondering what it will take to reach this town and to send out teams into other towns.

I thought of Tim, the pastor of a large church in New York. He has a vision to see his city transformed by the gospel. He is growing leaders and sending them out to plant churches. He is partnering with anyone he can find who is willing to plant gospel-centered churches. He has a heart for the cities of the world.

I thought of Gary, who runs his own business and in his spare time has a ministry to high school students. Forty of them have come to know Christ. Gary can't understand why his local church leaders are not embracing this work of God. He wonders what he should do next.

I'm writing for people like these. They and others like them have also been my teachers. As I've listened to their stories and the stories of countless others down through the ages, they have become my cloud of witnesses to the God revealed in Jesus and his mission in the world.

There is no formula, and there are no ten simple steps. We are workers in *God's* harvest field. We are utterly dependent on God for our salvation and for the results of our ministries. Nothing can explain the spread of the Christian movement throughout history other than the power of God that is present in the communication of the gospel of the crucified and risen Jesus Christ.[11]

What follows are the stories and lessons of our contemporaries and of those who have gone before us. They planted and they watered, but it is God who gave the growth.

1. White-hot faith

About three in the morning as we were continuing
instant in prayer, the power of God came mightily upon us,
insomuch that many cried out for exceeding joy and many
fell to the ground. As soon as we were recovered a little
from that awe and amazement at the presence of his
majesty we broke out with one voice, "We praise thee
O God; we acknowledge thee to be the Lord." [1]

John Wesley

A sixteen-year-old boy is taken captive by raiders and sold into slavery. Desperate with loneliness, hunger, and cold, he cries out for deliverance and God answers. He goes on to pioneer one of the greatest missionary movements the world has ever seen.

An obscure Augustinian monk agonizes over what it means to be made right with God through faith. His intense struggle is the catalyst for the Protestant Reformation.

A young minister returns from the mission field, a failure in his own eyes and devoid of the experience of God's loving acceptance. His heart is "strangely warmed" by the grace of God, and one of the most significant awakenings in modern history shakes Britain and spreads worldwide.

Patrick of Ireland, Martin Luther, and John Wesley—we remember them as powerful historical figures through whom God renewed the church and transformed the world. We honor them as heroes of the faith. We forget they began as broken men crying out to God for an encounter that would change their lives. Out of their personal encounters with God, these transformational leaders went on to renew the church and to shape the world in which we live.

For a number of years I have taught a church planting course for the Salvation Army in Sydney. I enjoy going back each year not only for the interaction with the students but also because of the location. The conference center sits on a hill above the northern beaches of Sydney overlooking the Pacific Ocean.

Sydney has the most expensive real estate in Australia, and every year one of the officers reminds me that the Salvation Army once owned the land for as far as the eye can see. In 1900, Miss Elizabeth Jenkins bequeathed hundreds of acres of farming land to the Salvation Army. Today that land would be worth hundreds of millions of dollars. The problem is that much of the land was carved up and sold off over the years for housing or was acquired by the state government for community use.

Every year I'm told, "Imagine what we could achieve if only we had that property today." The trap is set. We go back into the next session. Then I remind them that once the Salvation Army consisted of William and Catherine Booth sitting at their kitchen table, with no other resource than the call of God.

Church history is not made by well-financed, well-resourced individuals and institutions. History is made by men and women of faith who have met with the living God. Without faith it is impossible to please God.

I learned this lesson the hard way in our first church plant. Halfway through the second year, the church experienced intense conflict. I wondered how I would make it through. Since launching the new church, we had added a new family every week, and we were at over two hundred people. Naturally, as growth equals success, I thought I was the world's best church planter. Then a church fight erupted, and my world came crashing down.

I wanted to fight or run, and God just told me to stand.

Soon after, I heard John Wimber of the Vineyard movement say, "Jesus wants his church back." I realized that was my issue. Jesus wanted his church back, and he wanted me back.

I began seeking God like never before. I would rise early and go out into my garage, stoke up a small wood heater, and pray and read the Scriptures. This was not discipline; it was desperation. One morning alone in the garage, I had a strong sense of God saying, "It's not about just one new church; it's about a whole new generation of churches." From that moment, my calling has been to fuel church planting movements across Australia and beyond.

It took a few more months before peace was restored in our church. A few people left. Most stayed. God's blessing returned, but I was never the same again.

Profound encounters with God are important catalysts in the formation of movements for the renewal and expansion of the Christian faith. Social and political factors influenced the Protestant Reformation, but religious convictions and experiences centered on Jesus were the chief catalysts for change.

Valid experiences of God will be in harmony with his Word and must find expression in action. A white-hot faith is concerned with the Spirit, the Word, and the world. It aims to produce right-heart-edness, right thinking, and right action. It calls for the consecration of heart, head, and hands.[2]

Fresh encounters with God through the Word and the Spirit provide compelling authority that energizes a missionary movement to go and change the world.

The first Protestant missionary movement

I have only one passion, 'tis He, 'tis only He.[3]

Count Nikolas Zinzendorf

At the end of the seventeenth century, Protestantism in Europe was entering a religious ice age, frozen by passionless orthodoxy. One hundred and fifty years had passed since the death of Martin Luther, and still no significant missionary movement had emerged from the Reformation.

For centuries the religious orders—the Benedictines, Carmelites, Augustinians, Franciscans, and Dominicans—had been the well-spring of life for the renewal and expansion of the Catholic faith. In the regions they controlled, the Reformers abolished these orders without creating a functional equivalent. Protestantism was bereft of a mechanism for world missions until two young Moravians, one a potter and the other a carpenter, decided it was time to act.

When Leonard Dober and David Nitschmann set out to take the gospel to the West Indies in 1732, William Carey, the "father of Protestant missions," had not yet been born. Hudson Taylor, missionary pioneer, would not arrive in China for another one hundred and fifty years. Dober and Nitschmann were the first missionaries sent out by the Moravian Brethren. Within twenty years Moravian missionaries were in the Arctic among the Eskimos, in southern Africa, among the Indians of North America, and in Suriname, Ceylon, China, India, and Persia.

The Moravian Brethren originated in the Czech regions of Moravia and Bohemia in central Europe. They traced their roots back to the Czech reformer Jan Hus. The Roman Catholic Church condemned Hus as a heretic, and he was excommunicated and burned at the stake in 1415. Hus inspired the birth of the first Protestant church to break with Rome, one hundred years before Martin Luther. When the Reformation came, the Moravians forged links with the Reformers, including Luther and Calvin.

In the 1620s the Moravians lost the protection of the local nobility and suffered severe persecution by the Catholic Church. Their churches were closed, and they were hunted down and imprisoned. Some were tortured and executed, while others were forced into hiding or fled into exile. For the next one hundred years, the Moravian Brethren barely survived as an underground church—hardly the sort of people you would expect to launch a missionary movement.

The plight of the Moravians caught the attention of a young Austrian noble, Count Nikolaus Zinzendorf. As a young boy, Zinzendorf had devoted his life to Christ and the spread of the gospel throughout the world. In 1722 he opened his estate in Saxony as a sanctuary for the persecuted Moravians. With his help they built a village and called it Herrnhut, which meant "the Lord's watch." Zinzendorf set up a number of projects to serve this community. There was a bookshop, a dispensary, a school, and a printing press for cheap editions of the Bible and other literature.

By 1727 a steady stream of religious refugees had arrived—some with Lutheran, Reformed, Anabaptist, and even Catholic backgrounds. Each had a dream for the church restored; reality, however, proved to be quite different. It was hard for men and women who had suffered for their convictions to sacrifice those convictions for the sake of harmony. Factions developed, and this led to bitter disputes and broken relationships.

Zinzendorf was under pressure from local authorities to shut down this "hotbed of heresy." He could have relied on his power as a feudal lord to expel the warring factions. Instead, Zinzendorf stepped in to restore peace. He and his family moved out of their mansion into the village. He devoted all his time, energy, and wealth to serving the people. He spent long hours and days meeting with individuals and groups to restore harmony. He opened the Scriptures and helped the community to understand the mind of God.

Zinzendorf introduced structure into the community.

He appointed leaders on the basis of character and spiritual maturity. He drew up a set of forty-two statutes as the basis for community life. Zinzendorf divided the whole community into "bands." Each band consisted of two or three people of the same gender who met to open their hearts and to encourage, correct, and pray for one another. People were reconciled as they confessed their sins and made renewed commitments to live together in love. Night and day, Herrnhut became a center for prayer and worship.

By the summer of 1727 there was a "contagious and holy expectancy" at Herrnhut. Something wonderful was about to happen.

On August 13, 1727, the Moravians experienced what can only be described as a Pentecostal outpouring of the Holy Spirit as they celebrated the Lord's Supper. As the Spirit moved among them, their hearts were set on fire with new faith and love towards the Savior and with burning love towards one another. They embraced each other in tears. God breathed new life into their ancient movement.

Manifestations of the Holy Spirit's power continued, including divine healing. People met in small bands to confess their sins and pray for one another that they might be healed. The factions dissolved. Night watches and prayer vigils were established. Prayer was offered up around the clock, seven days a week, and continued uninterrupted for the next one hundred years.

This spiritual renewal was channeled into mission. Four years later the Count was visiting the court of the King of Denmark where he met Anthony Ulrich, an African slave from the West Indies. Ulrich had come to faith in Christ and met two Moravians at court. He poured out his heart to Zinzendorf as he described the shameful conditions of the slaves on the Danish island of St. Thomas. He spoke of his sister and brother and of their desire to hear the gospel. Zinzendorf was deeply moved and excited by the missionary challenge.

It was the following year when Leonard Dober, the potter,

and David Nitschmann, the carpenter, became the first Moravian missionaries. Zinzendorf spent the whole night before they left in prayer. He rose early and drove them in his carriage as far as he could. Before parting, they knelt by the roadside to receive his blessing. They carried their bundles on their backs as they walked away with just thirty shillings in their pockets. Zinzendorf had no other instructions to give them than "to do all in the Spirit of Jesus Christ."

Dober and Nitschmann had little understanding of what life would be like in the West Indies. They had no mission agency to support them. They had no example to follow. As they walked towards the port, they had no idea that they were clearing the way for the birth of the Protestant missionary movement.

These two young men became the founders of the Christian movement among the slaves of the West Indies. For the next fifty years the Moravians worked alone before any other Christian missionary arrived. By then the Moravians had baptized 13,000 converts and planted churches on the islands of St. Thomas, St. Croix, Jamaica, Antigua, Barbados, and St. Kitts.

Zinzendorf did not want to set up an independent Moravian church. His aim was to promote the unity of all Christians. Zinzendorf saw the Moravian movement as a missionary community, a church within the church, and all Moravians as "soldiers of the Lamb."[4]

The Moravians were the first Protestants to treat world missions as the responsibility of the whole church.[5] Under Zinzendorf, the Moravians became an intense and highly mobile missionary movement. Within two decades the Moravians sent out more missionaries than all Protestants had sent out in the previous two hundred years. The rapid deployment of so many young missionaries around the world was remarkable.

The outreach was made possible by a relative lack of concern with training, finances, or structure.[6] All of these missionaries were laypeople, mostly peasant farmers and tradesmen. They were trained as evangelists, not academic theologians. They received enough money to get to the port. The missionaries then worked for their passage across the ocean. On the mission field, they took up whatever work would provide enough food and clothing. They had no formal theological education, and they received scant training in language acquisition and cross-cultural ministry. Once they set sail, they had no financial support and no organization to look after them; there was no guarantee of health care, only the likelihood that they would never see their homeland again.

In the next 150 years, 2,158 Moravians volunteered to serve overseas. They went to the most remote, unfavorable, and neglected areas. This was something new in the expansion of Christianity: an entire Christian community—families as well as singles—devoted to world missions.[7]

The impact of the Moravians did not end with their own achievements. They profoundly influenced both William Carey, known as the "father of Protestant missions," and John Wesley, the founder of the Methodist movement. The Moravians prepared the way for the great Protestant missionary expansion of the nineteenth century. Christianity began the nineteenth century as a predominately European faith bound by traditionalism. By the end of the nineteenth century, Christianity was well on the way to becoming a truly global movement.

Zinzendorf described the members of the Moravian movement as "the Savior's happy people." The rallying cry of the Moravian missionary movement was: "May the Lamb that was slain receive the reward of his sufferings." Only the Moravians' supreme happiness in the Lamb can explain the freedom they had to sacrifice everything to carry the power and the fellowship of the crucified Christ across the world.[8]

When the Spirit comes with power

*The kingdom of heaven belongs to the violent who lay
hold upon it. But this violence is not accepted by God
unless the person practicing it is ready himself to bear
the shock in return. Whoever wrestles with God
in prayer puts his whole life at stake.*[9]

Jacques Ellul

In the history of the church it has been spiritual experiences that
have given birth to movements of renewal and expansion.

April 9, 2006, marked one hundred years since the Azusa Street
revival catapulted Pentecostalism onto the world stage. William
Seymour, the 34-year-old son of former slaves, led this revival. Early
Pentecostalism emphasized the "baptism of the Holy Spirit"
evidenced by speaking in tongues and the restoration of the true
church before Jesus returns. The emotionally charged meetings ran
all day and into the night. There was no central coordination of the
meetings, and Seymour rarely preached. He taught the people to cry
out to God for sanctification, the baptism with the Holy Spirit, and
divine healing.[10]

Immediately, missionaries fanned out from Azusa Street to the
world. Within two years they had brought Pentecostalism to parts
of Asia, South America, the Middle East, and Africa. They were
poor, untrained, and unprepared. Many died on the field. Their
sacrifices were rewarded; the Pentecostal/charismatic movement
became the fastest growing and most globally diverse expression
of worldwide Christianity.

Some researchers predict that, at the current rate of growth,
there will be one billion Pentecostals by 2025, most of them in Asia,
Africa, and Latin America.[11] Pentecostalism is perhaps the fastest
expanding movement—religious, cultural, or political—ever.
Communism, fascism, and militant Islam shaped the last century,
but none of them matched the impact of Pentecostalism.

Pentecostals are often identified with the high-profile individuals who appear on religious television in the United States. The reality is that the vast majority of Pentecostals live in the global South, or the developing world. The regions of Africa, Asia, and South America where Pentecostalism is growing the fastest also have the world's youngest and fastest-growing populations. If there is a "typical" Pentecostal, it is a poor woman living in a Nigerian village or a Brazilian shantytown.[12] Such people are the new face of Christianity, and they are also its future.

The Pentecostals' faith has a very down-to-earth influence in the developing world. An increasing volume of sociological research from Venezuela, to Jamaica, to Ghana, is showing how evangelical Christianity is remaking the lives of the poor—spiritually, morally, and materially. Pentecostalism in particular is proving more potent than government programs and social movements in improving the lives of the poor and marginalized.[13]

Religious zeal launched this staggering global expansion of Pentecostalism. What began as a revival meeting has become a global missionary movement. Pentecostalism reminds us that to change the world, we must first be changed. As we look at the birth and renewal of Christian movements, there are two means by which God develops white-hot faith in us. They are *crisis* and *process*. In the moment of crisis, we must learn to surrender to the grace of God. We must also learn to practice spiritual disciplines; this practice is the process that deepens our life in God.

Crisis: a surrendered life

The truck arrived at the house we were renovating. The concrete pour was on. Three carpenters and their laborer downed tools and each grabbed a wheelbarrow. I was the laborer. We had just twenty minutes to empty the truck of its load. After that time the driver would expect payment for every minute he waited. The pace was frantic. Wheelbarrows were lined up waiting to be filled.

Wet concrete is heavy and unstable. I took off down the driveway with a full load. I ran around the side of the house, through the mud to the back where we were laying the foundations for an extension. I braced myself for the last challenge—getting my wheelbarrow down a slippery plank and under the house to drop my load.

Just as I was about to take the plunge, I heard the booming voice of the foreman: "Watch out! We don't have a good laborer here."

I made it down the plank, emptied the wheelbarrow, and headed back up around the house to pick up my next load. Choking back the emotions, I felt totally beaten. "We don't have a good laborer here." The church plant wasn't coming together like I'd hoped. Personally, we had a couple of financial crises every week. We had two young children and one on the way. The strain was showing in our marriage, and I was barely holding it together. But I was right in the center of God's will and purpose. I had nowhere to run.

By the time I made it back up to the truck, I had determined in my heart there was no going back. I would stay the course. I would surrender my life and future to God and trust him with the outcome of my ministry.

This was to be the first of half a dozen opportunities over the next eighteen months to come to the place of surrender. I thought once would be enough. God had other plans.

Throughout the Scriptures, when God takes the initiative to call a person to his service it is often through a powerful encounter. Here are some examples: Jesus' baptism and wilderness experience; the transformation of the disciples at Pentecost; and Paul's encounter with Christ on the Damascus road. These were all "crisis" experiences. God intervenes in the midst of desolation and seeks a response. This pattern continues throughout the history of the Christian movement. Deep experiences of surrender precede revelation of God's purposes and the outpouring of power to achieve his will.

At the point of surrender, we renounce dependence on anything but the presence and power of God. All we bring is our brokenness and our need. It is God who initiates, and it is God's grace that transforms.

Experiences of crisis, surrender, and empowerment are scattered throughout the stories of every missionary movement. They touch the lives of founders and empower ordinary people to do extraordinary things. As people learn to go to the cross and find God there, they witness the power of the resurrection and the coming of the Holy Spirit. Those realities are the foundation out of which they minister.

Process: a disciplined life

The other dimension of cultivating a white-hot faith is *process*—the disciplined life. Spiritual disciplines may vary from movement to movement, but they are all activities that deepen our relationship with God.

The early followers of Christ met regularly to read the Scriptures and hear the teaching of the apostles. They met for prayer and to share the Lord's Supper; they also confessed their sins to one another. Spiritual disciplines were integrated into the rhythm of their lives. Every dynamic movement finds its unique mix of spiritual disciplines.

The monastic movement practiced "lectio divina" or prayerful reflection on the Scriptures. At the heart of the Jesuit order were the Spiritual Exercises of Ignatius Loyola, which were thirty days of prayerful meditation on the life, ministry, and death of Jesus. The Moravians and Methodists had classes and bands—accountability groups for prayer and the confession of sin. Members of the Student Volunteer Movement valued "the morning watch"—a daily time of Bible study and devotional prayer. Evangelicals are known for their expositional preaching and teaching of the Scriptures. Pentecostals place high value on experiencing God in corporate worship.

No movement can be sustained on crisis experiences alone. Spiritual disciplines prepare the way for, and support, life-changing experiences.

All the great movement pioneers learned both to surrender to God in crisis and to seek his grace through the practice of spiritual disciplines. Their secret is the joy they experience as they discover that Christ is sufficient. They are the men and women of whom the world is not worthy (Heb. 11:38). They have conquered nations, fed the poor, crossed oceans, climbed mountain ranges, and endured persecution, imprisonment, and death—all for the sake of the gospel. Their fellowship is with Jesus in his sufferings and in his joy. They display white-hot faith.

Jesus and white-hot faith

When they saw the courage of Peter and John,
and realized that they were unschooled, ordinary men,
they were astonished and they took note that these
men had been with Jesus.

Acts 4:13

At the birth of the Christian movement, we don't find its founder in the Temple at Jerusalem impressing the scholars with his learning and piety. We don't find him at the head of crowds of supporters who are impressed with his power to heal the sick and cast out demons. He's not wooing kings and governors.

Jesus was alone in the wilderness—hungry, thirsty, and weary from the battle with Satan. He was the obedient Son, waiting in the presence of his Father. Humble, dependent, broken, needy. Every support had been taken away. Every consolation had gone. There was only the cost of obedience and abandonment and the horrifying prospect of the cross.

Each temptation was an attack on his Sonship. Each temptation sought to have Jesus prove his identity through miraculous power rather than dependence, obedience, and suffering. Jesus prevailed and returned victorious over evil, but the battle with Satan continued throughout his public ministry until the final defeat of evil on the cross.

It was in the place of desolation that Jesus' identity and call were tested. He refused to take charge of his destiny. He chose the path of obedience. This second Adam triumphed over the tempter and led the way for all who would follow. Here is the foundation stone of the Christian movement. It is the heart of Jesus surrendered to the Father. Jesus was satisfied in the Father's love and purpose. All else was forsaken.

Jesus repeatedly withdrew to be alone with the Father in prayer—early in the morning, up on the mountainside, in the desert, and sometimes for a whole night. He prayed when he was under great strain. He prayed when he had important decisions to make. He prayed as he faced the prospect of crucifixion. He prayed on the cross itself.

The love of God was so real to Jesus, so compelling, that when he turned to God in prayer, the cry that naturally came to his lips was *Abba*, the Aramaic word for father. No other Jew had ever spoken of God as Abba, but Jesus always addressed God in this way, and he taught his disciples to do the same.[14]

Jesus taught his followers to expect the same intimacy with the Father and the same power to be witnesses to the ends of the earth. Before they could experience the power of God, they had to face their utter dependence on him. When Jesus called Simon, Andrew, James, and John, they were in a position of helplessness. They had fished all night and caught nothing. At the command of Jesus, they let down their nets one more time and hauled in a miraculous catch. As a result, Peter was overwhelmed by the presence of God in Jesus. He fell at Jesus' feet and confessed his unworthiness and his sin. He left his fishing boat and his business partners and followed Jesus immediately and unconditionally. His reaction reminds us of the Old Testament prophets who received their calls as they were overwhelmed in the presence of God.[15]

In Acts, the religious leaders saw the boldness of the early disciples, and they were amazed, for Peter and John were "uneducated, ordinary men." What set Peter and John apart? They had been with Jesus (Acts 4:13). The disciples' transformation from a scattered band of defeated and despairing men into the leaders of a dynamic missionary movement was achieved through their shared experience of the risen Son and his Holy Spirit. The expansion of early Christianity was more than a social phenomenon or human enterprise. It was the Lord himself who "added" believers to the church when the gospel was preached (Acts 2:47).

The apostle Paul was a well-educated, intelligent, and determined man. He boasted of his religious pedigree and accomplishments, but these attributes were nothing to him compared to the power of knowing Christ. His encounter on the Damascus road was all about relinquishing his abilities and credentials and surrendering to the Risen Christ.

Paul told the Corinthians that the troubles he experienced had pushed him beyond his ability to endure. Yet in the midst of despair he experienced the comfort of God and the power of God (2 Cor. 1:3-11). Paul's troubles taught him that the treasure of the gospel is carried in fragile jars of clay; this truth emphasized that the gospel's power comes from God alone, not from the messenger (2 Cor. 4:7-12).

You can run an institution with systems of command and control, but Jesus founded a movement. He brought his followers into the same experience he had with God the Father and God the Holy Spirit. He sent them to the ends of the earth with nothing but the message of salvation and the reality of God's power. A passionate faith is at the heart of every dynamic missionary movement. It is the greatest resource. Today, where Christianity is expanding rapidly in the developing world, it is often the only resource.

Christianity goes South

*As I travel, I have observed a pattern, a strange
historical phenomenon of God "moving" geographically
from the Middle East, to Europe to North America
to the developing world. My theory is this:
God goes where he is wanted.*[16]

Philip Yancey

For the last five hundred years the story of Christianity has been
bound up with Europe and European-derived cultures. Historian
Philip Jenkins records how over the past century the center
of gravity in the Christian world has shifted southward to Africa,
Asia, and Latin America.[17] These are the regions in which the largest
and fastest-growing Christian communities on the planet are found.
They are also the regions of fastest population growth. If these
trends continue, by 2050, only about one-fifth of the world's three
billion Christians will be non-Hispanic whites. While Northern
Hemisphere Christianity is in decline, a new era of Southern Christianity has dawned.

Let's take a look at Africa. In 1900, colonial Africa had a population of 108 million people, of whom 8.7 million, or 9 percent,
were Christian. The majority of those Christians were Coptic and
Ethiopian Orthodox. They were outnumbered by 34.5 million
Muslims—a ratio of 4:1.

By 1962, after Africa had shaken off colonial rule, there were
about 145 million Muslims and 60 million Christians—a ratio
of about 5:2. By 1985 a major expansion of the Christian faith had
taken place in the midst of the pessimism and turmoil of post-inde-
pendent Africa. The churches were often the only viable structures
remaining after the breakdown of state institutions. Ironically,
Christian African converts came predominantly from the poor and
marginalized. There were over 16,500 conversions a day and
an annual growth of six million people.[18]

African Muslims and Christians (millions).[19]

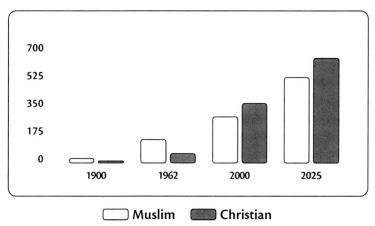

700
525
350
175
0

1900   1962   2000   2025

☐ Muslim ■ Christian

By 2000 there were 360 million Christians in Africa. David Barrett estimated that in the year 2000, 40.6 percent of Africans were Muslim and 45 percent were Christian. From 1900 to 2000 the ratio of Muslims to Christians shifted from four to one to less than one to one. If current trends continue, by 2025, there could be 633 million Christians in Africa, making it the second largest Christian continent after South America.[20]

Southern Christians, whether they are Catholic, Evangelical, or Pentecostal, are far more conservative in beliefs and in moral teaching than the Christians in the prosperous North. Christians of the global South have a supernatural view of the world and are more interested in personal salvation than in radical politics. They take the Bible seriously. They are more likely to believe that what they read in the gospels is happening in their midst. They believe that the world of the apostles is a present reality. Jenkins observed, "If there is a single area of faith and practice that divides Northern and Southern Christians, it is the matter of spiritual forces and their effects on the everyday human world."[21]

Two years ago I was working hard at home on an article about the incredible spread of the Christian faith in the developing world. Someone rang the doorbell, and I was a little annoyed at the interruption. Reluctantly I opened the door to face two Chinese people who wanted to tell me about Jesus. As we talked I discovered they were missionaries to Australia from Communist China. Eventually I returned to my writing with a living reminder that a new era has dawned in world missions.

Fifty years ago the fledgling church in China was reeling from the expulsion of Western missionaries and from persecution following the Communist takeover. Now fervent Chinese Christians are on my doorstep. Today the Chinese, Koreans, Indians, Brazilians, Nigerians, and many others are the rising force in world missions.

British author Martin Robinson talks about some of the church planters from the developing world he has met in the West.[22] They come from Haiti, Brazil, Ethiopia, Columbia, Mexico, Nigeria, and the Dominican Republic, to name a few. They often work, send money home to their extended families, and plant a church at the same time. They are mechanics, cab drivers, and laborers. Their hard work, faith, commitment, and exuberance are infectious.

The center of gravity for the Christian faith has moved south. Again, renewal and expansion has come from the fringes.

Trajectory of the Statistical Center of Global Christianity, AD 33-2100[23]

God chooses what appears to be weak and foolish to shame what appears to be powerful and wise (1 Cor. 1:25). Faith moves mountains.

Conclusion

White-hot faith is the fuel that missionary movements run on. Nothing happens without a deep dependence on God. Nothing leads us into a healthy dependence on the power of God more than to come face to face with our desperate need of him. Jesus is the Apostle and Pioneer of our faith. He led the way for us in surrender to the will of God and the power of the Holy Spirit.

White-hot faith is an important factor whenever we see great advances in the spread of the Christian faith. The stories of the Moravians and the Pentecostals illustrate its impact. The great movements of the Christian faith are only unleashed through the presence and power of God in the midst of his people who are faithful to his Word, led by his Spirit, and engaged in his mission. It is his harvest field. We are not passive bystanders but active participants in what God is doing. We plant and we water, but God gives the growth.

2. Commitment to a cause

While women weep as they do now, I'll fight.
While little children go hungry as they do now, I'll fight.
While men go to prison in and out, in and out, I'll fight.
While there yet remains one dark soul without the light
of God, I'll fight. I'll fight to the very end.

William Booth, founder of the Salvation Army

In September 1980, a 37-year-old electrician named Lech Walesa climbed over the barbed wire fences of the Lenin Shipyards in Gdansk, Poland, to join his comrades in their opposition to communist oppression. Ten years later, Walesa was elected president of Poland, and in East Germany the Berlin Wall had crumbled under the onslaught of demonstrators as border guards looked on. The grip of communism on the Soviet Union and its satellite states was broken. The Marxist dream of a communist utopia was no longer credible even to party members. A more compelling vision of a society built on individual freedom won the day.

It was not superior military might that defeated the communist empire. The authorities could have imprisoned and executed their opponents, as they had done in the past. They still had the power to unleash a nuclear nightmare. Communism dissolved as quickly as it had once emerged, but this second revolution took place with hardly a shot fired. Victor Hugo wrote, "There is one thing stronger than all the armies in the world, and that is an idea whose time has come."[1]

Movements that change the world deal with the ultimate issues. They are causes that make demands on followers. Apathy changes nothing, and it is the surest sign that a movement, organization, or society is in decline. Change takes place because people care enough to act on their deeply held beliefs. They choose "to live divided no more."[2]

Power does not finally depend on military or economic might but upon the ability to mobilize people around a cause.[3] Surprisingly, an eighteenth-century Anglican clergyman provides a very good example of this principle.

The Methodist revolution

In 1737 a defeated and depressed Anglican missionary to the American colonies returned home to England. He despaired, saying, "I went to America, to convert the Indians; but oh! who shall convert me?"[4] The name of the missionary was John Wesley, founder of the Methodist movement.

Through his contact with Moravian missionaries, Wesley saw the inadequacy of his own faith. He did not know the grace of God. He did not have the Moravians' joy and freedom in following Christ.

In his journal entry of May 24, 1738, he described how he went unwillingly to a Moravian gathering at Aldersgate Street in London where they were studying the book of Romans. It was a quarter to nine, and as the leader was describing the change that God works in the heart through faith in Christ, Wesley felt his heart "strangely warmed." He wrote, "I felt I did trust in Christ alone for salvation; and an assurance was given me that He had taken away my sins, even mine, and saved me from the law of sin and death."[5]

What Wesley had sought to achieve in his own strength—assurance of salvation and power for living—he now received through dependence on God. The change in John Wesley unleashed one of the greatest movements in the history of the church.

Fired by his encounter with God at Aldersgate, Wesley traveled Britain with a vision to convert and disciple the nation and to renew the languishing church. In his own words, his mission was "to reform the nation, by spreading scriptural holiness over the land."[6] His goal was to establish a movement of people who were learning to obey Christ and to walk as he did.

Soon Wesley was preaching to huge crowds. Wesley's intensity of commitment led to conflict with the Church of England. He preached in church buildings when local clergy gave their permission, but often he was forced to follow the example of his friend George Whitefield and take the gospel to the open air. When Wesley was forbidden to speak in his father's former parish church, he stood outside on his father's tombstone and preached to thousands. He declared, "The world is my parish!" By that he meant the clergy had no authority to keep him out of "their" parishes.

Wesley was not interested in just attracting crowds. As a brilliant strategist and innovator, he created and adapted structures that strengthened and united his followers in a rapidly expanding movement. What set Wesley apart was not the gospel he preached but his ability to gather converts into a disciplined movement. He wrote in his journal: "The devil himself desires nothing more than this, that the people of any place should be half-awakened and then left to themselves to fall asleep again. Therefore, I determine by the grace of God not to strike one stroke in any place where I cannot follow the blow."[7]

Wesley multiplied a variety of groups—classes, bands, and societies—to bring individuals to conversion and then to ensure their progress in discipleship.

The requirement for joining a Methodist class was "a desire to flee from the wrath to come." Most conversions took place in the classes rather than through the field preaching. The classes were also the disciplinary unit of the movement. Inquiry was made into the state of each member's soul, and unrepentant offenders were removed from the fellowship. Howard Snyder describes the classes as "house churches" meeting in the various neighborhoods where people lived. The class leaders (both men and women) were pastors and disciplers.[8]

All Methodists were class members. Those who were clearly converted moved on to join the "bands." While the major focus of the class was on conversion and discipline, the focus of the band was confession and pastoral care. The "societies" were composed of all class and band members within a local area.

Wesley refused to preach Christian doctrine without discipline. He believed that there could be no true Christianity without both. Methodism was a place to find support and accountability in the struggle against sin. A Methodist could not give up the fight and remain in the movement for very long. Wesley thought it was better to lose members than to lose discipline. He wrote that to preach like an apostle without joining converts together to learn the ways of God "is only begetting children for the murderer."[9]

In 1748 Wesley visited the Bristol Methodist society and expelled 170 of its 900 members. He removed them for reasons that included smuggling, cursing, drunkenness, wife beating, and quarreling.[10] Wesley's actions sound harsh to our ears. It helps us understand why Wesley polarized people in his own day. Today his commitment to holiness would have had him branded as a dangerous fundamentalist—which is probably why movement leaders are only made "saints" *after* they have died.

Wesley never used his power over the Methodist movement for personal gain. His strict discipline came from a deeply held conviction regarding the seriousness of sin and the imminent judgment of God. He really believed that people were lost without Christ. He really believed that sin brought destruction in this life and the next. He also believed that faith in Christ could, and should, result in loving obedience to his commands.

Through this system of classes, bands, and societies, Methodists united to encourage each other, confess their sins, pray for each other, and hold one another accountable for their progress in the faith. Without this system for the care and mobilization of Methodist converts, Wesley would have only been known as a great evangelist, second to Whitefield. Instead he founded a movement that far exceeded his own personal achievements.

Wesley not only reached the masses of people who were outside of the Anglican church, he turned thousands of them into workers committed to the cause of Methodism—traveling preachers, group leaders, educators, and visitors of the sick and of prisoners. Every Methodist was expected to have a ministry. At least one in ten had a formal leadership position in the movement. Many of those leaders were women, including some of Wesley's preachers.

Opponents among the Anglican clergy condemned this "prostituting of the ministerial function" and mocked the poor and illiterate Methodists who "pretended to be pregnant with a message from the Lord."[11] To Wesley, they were ministers of the gospel. He took an intense interest in their development. Wesley examined his leaders and preachers every year to ensure their commitment, their character, their faith, and their effectiveness. Methodists were issued "tickets of membership" that were renewed quarterly. Discipline and accountability at every level became a key distinctive of the Methodist movement.

Wesley was able to inspire commitment to the Methodist cause because he embodied that commitment. He endured opposition and derision from his peers in the church and in society. He defied the violence of the mobs that turned up to disrupt his meetings. He lived an austere lifestyle and shunned every distraction to his calling. He endured the strain of constant travel on horseback and of long, hard days of work. He traveled almost a quarter of a million miles on horseback, preached 40,000 sermons, and saw over 100,000 conversions. By the end of his life there were 71,463 Methodists in Britain and 61,811 in the United States.[12]

Methodism was well on the way to becoming a worldwide movement. Today there are over 33 million Methodists worldwide and many more in the movements that Wesley inspired.

Although there were many factors that fed into this amazing expansion, none were more important than Methodists' discipline and commitment to their cause. Commitment to the cause is the currency that movements trade in. It's the air they breathe, the reason they exist.

Cultivating commitment

Dynamic religious movements are clear about what they believe and why they exist. They don't confuse their beliefs with the beliefs of other faiths. They only admit and retain members who are fully committed to the beliefs and practices of the movement. They build strong ties between members for mutual support and accountability.

Like most movements, Methodism eventually drifted from high levels of commitment to leniency. Its clergy professionalized. Its members were more refined. Methodism became an accepted institution of society and lost its evangelistic zeal. Practices such as the confession of sin in accountability groups faded away.

Once commitment wanes, it is almost impossible to recover.[13] Three factors enable a movement to maintain a strong commitment to its cause: founding charism, alignment, and medium tension.

a.   Founding charism: unique identity and calling

To survive, every living thing is both constantly changing and constantly remaining the same. If an organism doesn't do both, it ceases to exist. Living organisms are constantly seeking self-renewal by referring back to their essential identity and adapting to their environment.[14] Likewise, movements must adapt to their changing environment while remaining true to their identity. (We will return to this topic when we look at "Adaptive Methods" in Chapter Five.)

The Catholic religious orders refer to their unique identity and mission as their "founding charism"—their founding gift of grace.[15] The most effective religious orders remain true to their founding charism even while they adapt to a changing world.

Effective movements know who they are. They know their founding charism and safeguard it over time. Their methods may change, but the cause never does. A clear identity and agenda for change create a tension between the ideal promoted by a movement and current reality. Transformational change is the outcome of that tension.

Wesley's cause was the conversion and discipling of a nation, the renewal of a fallen church, and "scriptural holiness" spread throughout the land. He built everything around this central purpose and adapted structures and strategies to serve it.

Over time every movement wanders from its founding charism and can only be renewed by returning to it in a fresh way. That return must be both true to the movement's unique calling and innovative in how that calling is lived out.[16]

b.   Commitment mechanisms: alignment

Having a clear identity and mission is only the beginning. Every aspect of the movement must be aligned with its overriding purpose. Wesley's system of classes, bands, and societies ensured that he not only made converts but also channeled them into a disciplined and focused movement. His discipline of wayward members and regular examination of local leaders and circuit riders ensured commitment was maintained.

Effective movements develop "commitment mechanisms" that ensure corporate and individual behavior is aligned with identity and purpose.[17] Commitment mechanisms include strong relational ties, personal sacrifice, and the expectation of obedience to the norms of the group.

Researchers Jim Collins and Jerry Porras discovered that the truly great companies fostered a commitment to an ideology that was pervasive throughout the organization. For these companies, alignment was built into the selection and training of new staff, the screening out of staff who did not fit with the ideology, and the promotion of those who did. These companies also actively promoted strong social bonds within the organization. They found alignment around a clear ideology enabled the best companies to turn their people loose to experiment, change, adapt, and—above all—to act.[18]

This is precisely what Wesley achieved. The Methodist cause was clear and reinforced by every aspect of Methodist life. Only those who remained committed to the cause remained within the movement. They poured their lives, their creativity, their time, and their money into a cause they deeply believed in. This context of commitment empowered the Methodists to take the gospel to the ends of the earth.

c.   Medium tension: distinct but connected

Commitment to a cause attracts both admiration *and* opposition. Methodism attracted its fair share of ridicule from genteel society and violence from the mobs.

Confrontation strengthens the resolve and unity of members within a movement, but there are limits to how high levels of commitment can become before they isolate a movement from the surrounding culture. Successful movements find the "medium tension" point with the surrounding environment.[19] Commitment levels are high, but not so high that potential members view joining the movement as a total break with their relationships and culture.

It is possible for a religious faith to be so alien to its surrounding culture as to make conversion highly unlikely, except for a limited number of social outsiders and misfits. If a movement is regarded as too deviant, it may only recruit those who are relationally isolated. However, unless a religious movement is demanding and different, it will not be taken seriously as a religious alternative. Movements must maintain a balance between conformity and deviance, and between innovation and continuity within a culture or social network.[20] What did this medium tension look like for Wesley?

Surprisingly, Wesley remained an Anglican his whole life. He loved the Anglican Church. His Methodist societies functioned as a renewal movement within Anglicanism and only became a separate denomination after his death. As a movement, Methodism was free to act without the constraints of the Anglican system. Methodism was able to attract committed followers who were alienated from the more respectable but lukewarm mainstream religion. By remaining within Anglicanism, the Methodist societies were less likely to be seen as a deviant version of the Christian faith. They were distinct but connected to the culture around them. As a result, Methodism had the best of both worlds—high levels of member commitment *and* connection with the culture.

Christian Smith argues that American evangelicalism is both distinct and connected. He contrasts evangelicalism with both fundamentalism and liberal Protestantism, and he contends that what distinguishes evangelicalism is its "engaged orthodoxy." American evangelicals remain committed to orthodox Protestant theology and belief. They are distinct. At the same time, they confidently and proactively engage in the intellectual, cultural, social, and political life of the nation. They are connected.[21]

In contrast, fundamentalism is a form of Protestantism that is defensively separate from the surrounding culture. It is distinct but not engaged. As a result, fundamentalism is a movement turned in on itself, lacking vitality.

Liberal Protestants have chosen an even worse position. They are engaged with but not distinct from the prevailing culture. Their accommodation of the surrounding secular values lowers the tension with the culture but also weakens their ability to affect that culture. What remains for liberal Protestantism is the desire to reinterpret Christian faith with the categories, values, and commitments of the modern/postmodern world.

The key to evangelicalism's vitality is its ability to exist in tension with the surrounding culture while at the same time remaining engaged. Wesley maintained that tension, and so did Jesus.

Jesus and commitment to a cause

When Jesus calls a man, he bids him come and die![22]

Dietrich Bonhoffer

At the beginning of his ministry Jesus proclaimed, "The time has come. The kingdom of God is near. Repent and believe the good news!" Jesus' cause was the kingdom of God. The establishment of God's rule through Jesus was good news because it brought healing to the sick, deliverance from Satan and demons, the offer of forgiveness and a new relationship with God as Father, and the promise of eternal life.[23]

Jesus called for a response of repentance and faith. The foundation of discipleship was personal commitment to Jesus. Self-denial was the fruit of that commitment. The disciples left everything and lived a wartime lifestyle for the sake of the kingdom. Jesus expected conflict and persecution. A sense of urgency kept him and his followers moving from town to town.

What was Jesus' mission? Positively, he said that he came so that we might have life and have it to the full. He came into the world as a light so that anyone who believes in him should no longer live in darkness. He came to seek and save that which was lost.

Yet his mission not only brought light, life, and salvation, it also brought division and a sword. He came to bring fire on earth and longed for it to be kindled. He came to set a man against his father, a daughter against her mother, and a daughter-in-law against her mother-in-law. He came for judgment so that the blind would see, and those who can see would become blind.

Jesus demonstrated unwavering commitment to his mission. Before launching his public ministry, he won a private battle against

Satan's attempts to divert him from the true nature of his mission. He faced the continued scrutiny and opposition of the religious leaders. At the right time, he set his face to go to Jerusalem and die for the cause he championed. He died deserted by his closest companions.

Jesus expected the same unwavering commitment from his disciples. He expected his closest disciples to walk away from their livelihoods, to leave their homes behind, and to follow him. Fishermen dropped their nets, tax collectors closed their books, and husbands and fathers left their homes. He told one young man to sell all he had, give it to the poor, and follow him. Jesus challenged one disciple to choose between following him and burying his father.

Jesus told his disciples they could leave if he offended them. On one such occasion when some of his followers drifted away, offended by his teaching, he turned to Peter and asked, "Do you want to go too?" (John 6:60-70).

He allowed his disciples mistakes and failures, but he never softened his call to total commitment to the cause of the kingdom. Jesus expected his followers to make the same sacrifices and demonstrate the same commitment that he did. Only those willing to take up their cross and follow him could be his disciples. Their loyalty to him had to come before every other loyalty. He told his disciples that he was sending them out as sheep to the wolves. They would be hated, persecuted, and put in jail; some would even be killed. No disciple who turned back was worthy of him.

At the heart of Jesus' missionary movement were his closest disciples who traveled and ministered with him and who were sent out on missions. They gave up their normal occupations and left their homes to join his mobile missionary team. A wider circle of up to five hundred people remained in their normal life situations, although some traveled with Jesus for short periods. Beyond them were the crowds of thousands who were a mixture of opponents, onlookers, those seeking miracles, and potential disciples. Jesus intentionally ministered within each of these concentric circles, but he made it his highest priority to intensively teach and train the few who made up the committed core of his movement.

Jesus left the expansion of the Christian movement to his followers, who were filled with his Holy Spirit for that purpose. The church that emerged after Pentecost both attracted and repelled people. In Jerusalem, in the wake of God's judgment on Ananias and Sapphira, no one else dared join with the followers of Jesus, even though they regarded them highly. Yet paradoxically, Luke records that increasing numbers of men and women believed in the Lord and were added to the church (Acts 5:13-15).

The people of Jerusalem were aware of a clear distinction between those who believed in Jesus and those who didn't. They knew that they too could join the movement at any time but not without repentance and faith. There was something about the Jerusalem church that was attractive and at the same time dangerous.

The New Testament church had its share of failings, sins, and heresies, yet no New Testament writer regarded this situation as acceptable. Paul admonished the Galatians for abandoning the gospel. He assigned anyone who preached another gospel to eternal condemnation. He warned the Corinthians not to indulge in idolatry and sexual immorality, or, like the Israelites, they would face God's judgment. Likewise, the writer of Hebrews called for perseverance under persecution and reminded his readers of the dangers of ignoring the discipline of God. Peter warned against false teachers in the church who were bringing destruction on themselves. John, in his epistle of love, wrote against those who had left the church, denying that Jesus is the Christ. He made it clear that those who deny the Son also deny the Father. He labeled those who teach such things as "antichrists." The book of Revelation begins with a series of letters to the churches with encouragements and warnings to stay true to the gospel in both doctrine and behavior. The risen Christ declares, "Those whom I love I rebuke and discipline. So be earnest, and repent!" (Rev. 3:19).[24]

Clearly, the church of the New Testament continued in the pattern that Jesus established of expecting faithfulness to the gospel in doctrine and behavior. There is grace and discipline for those who stray, but warnings, rebuke, and expulsion for those who show contempt for the riches of God's kindness.

Jesus' call to discipleship clashes with every culture and every human heart. In the West, it confronts our modern/postmodern individualism. We are uncomfortable with a God who makes demands of us. We are uncomfortable with the idea that the Creator of the universe might have an opinion on how we should conduct ourselves. We recognize no other authority than ourselves. We do not easily come under the authority of the Scriptures or accountability to the body of Christ.

The call to commitment is hard for us to hear. It creates tension with the world around us. Both grace and truth are required to rescue a lost world.

Why Sydney Anglicans are unpopular

> *What we suffer from today is humility in the wrong place. Modesty has moved from the organ of ambition. Modesty has settled upon the organ of conviction, where it was never meant to be. A man was meant to be doubtful about himself, but undoubting about the truth; this has been exactly reversed.*[25]

G.K. Chesterton

The Anglican diocese of Sydney is one of the most conservative evangelical dioceses in the world. It has been that way since British settlement in 1788. Meanwhile the rest of the Anglican Church and Australian society has changed. Sydney Anglicans have adapted their forms and methods, but they refuse to alter their convictions about the truth of Scripture and the gospel. Sydney Anglicans are a movement within Anglicanism.

One of the indicators that Sydney Anglicans are a movement is the strong reaction they provoke from the press and even from other Anglicans. One Anglican critic labeled them "fundamentalists" who are narrow, rigid, and ideological in their approach to life, the Scriptures, and the church. An Anglican theologian described them as "spiritually dangerous for the health of church and society" and called them to repent of their narrow mindset.[26] Movements clearly define who they are and have an agenda for change. That brings them into tension with others.

There are more socially acceptable mainstream churches in Australia than the Sydney Anglicans. Nobody is upset with them, and nobody takes them seriously. Declining religious institutions sin by "omission." It's what they *don't* do that is the problem. Movements sin by "commission"—it's what they *do* that upsets everyone.

Outside of the Sydney diocese, Australian Anglicanism faces serious and worsening decline. Half of all Anglican adult attenders are over sixty years old.[27] Soon the largest age category for the Anglican church attenders will be 70-79 years old. Members are dying, and they are not being replaced. Whatever the future of Australian Christianity is, it will not be Anglican, unless it is Sydney Anglican.

In contrast with other dioceses, the Sydney Anglicans are ordaining record numbers of clergy and showing healthy growth in attendances, new congregations, and new churches. It seems ordinary Australians respond well to these "dangerous fundamentalists."

What makes Sydney Anglicans different? At the heart it is their unwavering commitment to what they believe and their willingness to turn that belief into action.

A good example is the Ministry Training Scheme (MTS). The scheme offers apprenticeship training in Bible-centered ministry in churches across Australia. The stated purpose of MTS is "to train men and women who can declare the saving work of Christ in the world."[28] Participants are recruited from the best young leaders in the dioceses. MTS looks for leaders who can break new ground for the gospel and train others to do the same. Classroom academics need not apply.

MTS takes both hands-on ministry and theological training seriously. Interns spend most of their time engaged in evangelism, youth ministry, leading conferences and camps, and teaching and pastoring small discipleship groups. They learn how to present the gospel both one-on-one and in small and large groups. Every intern is encouraged to start something new—ideally among non-Christians.

MTS develops long-term partnerships with churches and pastors who provide apprentices with ministry experience, training, and mentoring. Interns are paid a basic allowance by their church that enables them to commit to the program full time. Each week interns meet with a qualified pastor-trainer to review their ministry and reflect theologically. Pastor-trainers are chosen for their Bible-centered ministry and godly character.

Many apprentices end up at the diocese's Moore Theological College, where they begin their formal theological education as experienced and proven practitioners. Eventually they return to the field and become recruiters and trainers of new interns.

By 2006 there were 1,000 interns who had participated in the scheme, and about forty percent of them were women. In that year there were 240 interns placed in 88 churches or university ministries. Graduates now serve in the media and arts, in education, as pastors and church planters, and as cross-cultural missionaries in six different countries. No other diocese comes close to Sydney's achievement in growing the next generation of leaders. The price they pay for making a difference is that not everyone likes them.

Conclusion

Commitment does not guarantee the rightness of a cause, but it does determine the likelihood of any cause making a difference. Committed people make history. They live in alignment with their deeply held beliefs. Missionary movements build environments that sustain and reinforce commitment to the cause. They are in tension with the world around them because they have an agenda for change. They are also deeply connected with their world. It's the combination of connecting while remaining distinct that enables movements to make history and change the world.

3. Contagious relationships

Every real friendship is a sort of secession, even a rebellion.
. . . In each knot of Friends there is a sectional "public opinion"
which fortifies its members against the public opinion of
the community in general. Each therefore is a pocket
of potential resistance.[1]

C. S. Lewis

My dad's boyhood hero was his older cousin, Jim Spence. Jim grew up in the Australian outback. With the outbreak of World War II looming, Jim and six of his mates lied about their ages and joined the Australian Army. Jim was sixteen.

When war broke out, the boys went into combat in North Africa. Later they were redeployed to fight in the jungles of New Guinea, an island to the north of Australia. As a young teenager, my father would eagerly await news of Jim's wartime adventures.

Out of all his friends, Jim was the only one to come home alive. He returned as a hero and moved to Sydney to live with Dad's family. Jim became like an older brother to Dad. On hot nights they slept out on the balcony under the stars and smoked Jim's army ration of tobacco.

All was not well with Jim. He was deeply disturbed by his horrific wartime experiences. He became depressed and thought about suicide. One Sunday afternoon Jim hit rock bottom. He had been drinking, and he decided he would jump off the Sydney Harbor Bridge. As he made his way towards the harbor, he could hear singing and music. An evangelist was preaching in the open air. Jim understood that only God could rescue him, and he put his trust in Jesus—much to the horror of my father!

By now Dad was eighteen. He had cruised through high school doing as little work as possible and getting into plenty of trouble. His one love was playing rugby. He could not understand or accept that his war hero cousin had "gone religious." Jim invited Dad to different Christian meetings, but Dad wanted nothing to do with them.

A few months later Dad was in bed suffering from a bout of the mumps. Jim came to visit and challenged him about where his life was headed. Dad had witnessed the change in Jim who was now planning to return to the jungles of New Guinea, not as a soldier, but as a missionary. Through Jim's example, my father became aware that his own life was lacking meaning and purpose.

Finally, Dad agreed to go with Jim to hear an American evangelist. That night Dad gave his life to Christ at the meeting. He gave up rugby and began training to become a missionary, like Jim, to New Guinea. A few years later he completed theological training and married my mother. They sailed to New Guinea in 1951 as pioneer missionaries.

Jim spent the rest of his life as a missionary in New Guinea. My father spent the rest of his working life in ministry. After returning from missionary service, he was a pastor back in Australia then became the head of a Christian welfare agency.

Everything changed when Dad saw the transformation in Jim. Until then, Dad had no felt need for a faith of his own. Jim's dramatic conversion on the streets of Sydney is the exception. Dad's conversion through a close relationship is the rule. Like a virus, the gospel travels along these lines of preexisting contagious relationships.

The rise of Christianity

Finally, all questions concerning the rise of Christianity are one: How was it done? How did a tiny obscure messianic movement from the edge of the Roman Empire dislodge classical paganism and become the dominant faith of Western civilization?[2]

Rodney Stark

From one of the earliest recorded attacks on Christianity, we learn something about the nature of its expansion. Celsus, a second century Greek philosopher, alleged that Christianity was the faith of uneducated slaves, women, and children. He complained it was spread from house to house "by wool workers, cobblers, laundry workers, and the most illiterate and bucolic yokels" who claimed that they alone knew the right way to live.[3]

By AD 40 the movement Jesus founded had about 1,000 followers. By 300 AD the number had grown to around six million people or about ten percent of the population of the Roman Empire.[4] Christianity's spread was fast and spontaneous; it happened without a centralized coordinating organization.

Only the Roman state rivaled Christianity in geographic spread and influence. Eventually, not even the power of Rome could stamp out this new faith. Even Rome had to make its peace with Christianity. Never has any movement—social, religious, or political—achieved such a rapid advance in a dominant culture without the aid of military force. How was it done?

In the first century, if you had a church gathering in your neighborhood, chances are you lived in a large port city that was also home to a Jewish community—Alexandria, Carthage, Corinth, Ephesus, Rome, or Thessalonica.[5]

At that time most Christians were Jewish, and their networks of friends and relatives were Jewish. Hellenistic Jews (Greek in language and culture) living outside of Israel were the most responsive people in the Empire to the Christian gospel. They had weaker ties to their traditional faith, and they were open to new ideas. The Apostle Paul fulfilled his mission to the Gentiles by first reaching these Jews in Gentile port cities. The network of Hellenistic synagogues throughout the Empire was the beachhead through which the gospel spread in depth.

What was true for Paul was also true of the great mass of ordinary Christians who spread the gospel throughout the Empire. They followed their social networks of relatives and friends, and reached the Hellenized Jews of the Diaspora (or Dispersion) living outside Israel.

History has focused on the achievements of the leading figures of the early church. These apostles, prophets, teachers, and evangelists played their part in knitting together a rapidly expanding movement, but they were the exception, not the rule. Overwhelmingly, early Christianity was not spread by "professionals" but by ordinary people whose names and deeds went unrecorded.

The Roman authorities sought to halt the expansion of Christianity by targeting its leadership. The pagan cults they were used to dealing with were elitist organizations, supported by the state and led by professional priests. The authorities assumed that if they chopped off the head the body would die. The approach of targeting Christian leaders did not work because early Christianity was a mass movement with a highly committed rank and file who were active in spreading the faith.[6]

Christian conversions followed networks of relationships. Missionaries often led the way, but their ministry focused on making initial contacts with members of a social group. Once some insiders were converted, they became the key to the gospel spreading throughout the rest of the social network, while the missionary played a more supportive role.[7]

No movement can sustain exponential growth if expansion is primarily the responsibility of paid professionals. Christianity grew exponentially through the efforts of ordinary people who were inspired and supported by missionaries such as Paul. That's why Celsus complained that the new faith was spread from house to house by wool workers, cobblers, laundry workers, and illiterate and bucolic yokels.

Celsus was right to be concerned. The most reliable predictor of conversion is relationships, especially preexisting, positive relationships. Conversion is a social phenomenon; it is often about accepting the faith of one's friends.[8] Whatever someone's prior beliefs, he is far more likely to adopt a new faith if he witnesses a friend or family member convert to that faith. As the number of recently converted friends and family increases, so does the likelihood of conversion.[9] The principle of contagious relationships reflects that God has made us, in his image, as social beings.

New religious movements fail when they become closed social networks. For continued exponential growth, a movement must maintain open relationships with outsiders, and it must also reach out into new, adjacent social networks. As open movements grow, their "social surface" expands exponentially. Each new member opens up new networks of relationships between the movement and potential members.[10] Contagious relationships are at the heart of the spread of every movement.

Early Christianity grew because converts maintained open relationships with the social worlds from which they came. If the church had responded to persecution and ridicule by becoming a closed, secretive sect, there is no way it could have continued to win new converts. Instead, the Christian faith continued to spread into adjacent social networks.[11]

The importance of social networks is true for the spread of all faiths, but Christianity had an advantage, inherited from Judaism—belief in one true God. Unless there is one true God, there is not much motivation for evangelism. When there are many gods, new gods are merely "supplements rather than alternatives."[12] New gods are added without the need to reject old ones. In the ancient world no one supposed that there was only one valid religion or only one true God, so there were no missionaries. Nor was there such a thing as "conversion."

Paganism is an inherently weaker faith because it accepts a variety of gods and beliefs. Only monotheism can generate the level of commitment to mobilize non-professionals in evangelism.[13] Non-exclusive religions cater to individualistic consumers who can choose from an array of options. Without monotheism, it is very difficult to build a communal faith with social strength. That's why paganism in the Greco-Roman culture had difficulty in getting anyone to do anything. There was no "church" of paganism. There was no missionary enterprise to take the "good news" of paganism to ends of the earth. In contrast, Christianity was able to channel members' commitment into building Christian community and taking the message of salvation to the world.

Judaism was also a monotheistic faith, but it never matched Christianity in reaching Gentiles. As a faith, it never fully escaped its ethnic nature. To fully convert to the Jewish faith, Gentiles had to become Jews. Christianity appealed to both Jews and Gentiles, Greeks and barbarians, men and women, slaves and free. It reached the poor and the ignorant, as well as the educated and the wealthy, with the simple message of the gospel.

Christianity appealed to all levels of society, and it spread rapidly through relational networks. It was able to generate an intense community of followers who were committed to a common cause. This cause proved more powerful than the state-sponsored religions, and even more powerful that the might of Empire.

Christianity conquered the Roman world without an organizational structure, without access to significant resources, without academic institutions, and without a professionalized clergy. Ordinary people, on fire with the love of Christ and empowered by the Holy Spirit, told their families, friends, and casual acquaintances what God had done for them.

By the fourth century, Rome had a Christian emperor in Constantine. Christianity came to occupy a position of privilege, backed by the Roman state. The church gained the power and resources it lacked, but it lost the intense commitment and missionary zeal of its members.

Principles of contagious relationships

Movements appear to grow spontaneously and randomly, but on closer inspection they are spreading within and across networks of relationships. Belief is a social phenomenon. Whether you're a Communist, a Manchester United fan, a Conservative, or an environmentalist, relationships play an important part in forming and maintaining your beliefs. Ideas spread like viruses, from person to person. In the age of mass communication, word of mouth is still the most important form of communication. Relationships are the key ingredient in the exponential growth of movements.

A study in the 1970s of American Pentecostalism showed that this movement was growing via face-to-face recruitment within pre-existing social networks. Wives came to faith when they saw the change in their husbands. Young adults converted soon after the conversion of a long-term friend. The stronger the social network, the faster Pentecostalism spread once it gained a foothold. In contrast, communities made up of disconnected individuals were unlikely to see rapid growth.[14]

There are many factors that influence the decision to adopt a new faith, but the most important factor is a close and positive relationship with a committed participant.[15] From a human point of view, conversion is accepting the opinion of your friends.[16] Mass meetings and dynamic leaders are not enough for effective recruitment, unless they play a role in motivating existing members to win over their social networks. The key to the spread of any movement is face-to-face recruitment by committed participants.[17]

Successful movements develop strategies to remain open social networks that are able to reach into new adjacent social networks and sustain exponential rates of growth. For a movement to grow rapidly it has to spread both *within* social networks and *between* social networks.

Here are three factors that contribute to how contagious a movement becomes.

1. The strength of weak ties

If you're looking for a job, forget about searching newspapers and the Internet; you should get out more and meet people. You're most likely to get your next job through your relationships—possibly through a friend, but more likely through an acquaintance. This phenomenon is called "the strength of weak ties."[18] Your close friends tend to link you with people you already know. By definition, acquaintances link you to a variety of untapped social networks. They expand your relational world.

Certain people act as the links within and between social networks. Malcolm Gladwell classifies these people as *connectors, mavens,* and *salesmen.*[19] Connectors have an extraordinary ability to make multiple friends and acquaintances across different networks. With a foot in so many different relational worlds, they bring people together.

Connectors are the people specialists, while mavens (Yiddish for someone who accumulates knowledge) are the information specialists. Mavens are the people you go to when you need information to make a decision. They love accumulating knowledge and communicating it to others.

Salesmen are the persuaders. They connect emotionally with others and convince them of the need to adopt new ideas or behaviors. These three types of people who share relationships, knowledge, and persuasion are the bridges over which new ideas spread contagiously from person to person and group to group. Movements know this intuitively and rarely spend vast amounts of money on advertising and mass communication.

2. Tight but open social networks

For a movement to grow, it must not only reach new people, it must retain them, *and* it must build them into a committed force for change. To do so, it is important to foster strong relationships *within* the movement. Movements made up of a collection of casual acquaintances will lack energy, commitment, and focus. A successful movement is a "tight" social network.

Yet, if a movement is too tight, it will become socially isolated; it may keep its members, but it will not grow. In closed groups, internal relationships can be so strong that they exclude significant relationships with outsiders. This social isolation limits the ability to recruit. Those who are recruited will tend to be isolated individuals without strong social networks. These individuals are unlikely to be the relational bridge that others cross to join the movement.

Growth can only continue if the movement remains a tight *and* open social network.[20] Effective movements maintain a balance between internal and external attachments. They retain the ability to reach out and into new adjacent social networks. By doing so, they are able to sustain exponential rates of growth.[21]

3. Just six handshakes away

In 1967 Harvard professor Stanley Milgram asked his students to help him find out how many acquaintances it takes to connect two randomly selected people.[22] Two names were chosen, and each student received a letter with the instructions:

- If you are acquainted with the person, mail it directly to them.
- If not, mail it to someone you know personally who is more likely than you to know the target.
- Have them do the same.

We are just six handshakes away from everyone on the planet.

Milgram and his students discovered that the most common number of intermediate persons was 5.5. In 1991 John Guare turned the idea into a play called *Six Degrees of Separation*.

Despite the complexity of our world, we are all just a few handshakes away from everyone else. Relationships and social networks will always be the most important human factor in the adoption of new ideas and the spread of movements that change the world.

Movements are social organisms more than they are organizations. Overlapping networks of relationships form their organizing structure. That should be no surprise since humanity is made in the image of God, and God is Father, Son, and Holy Spirit.

Jesus and contagious relationships

> *The first thing Andrew did was to find his brother*
> *Simon and tell him, "We have found the Messiah."*

John 1:41

Jesus knew the importance of relationships. From the beginning, the movement he founded grew through the favorable reports that spread from person to person.

Jesus recruited his band of disciples through relational networks. It was John the Baptist, Jesus' relative, who first connected Andrew to Jesus. Andrew went and found his brother Simon Peter to tell him he had met the Messiah. Jesus called Philip who was from Bethsaida, Andrew and Peter's town. Philip recruited Nathaniel, and James and John were fishermen together with Peter and Andrew.

Jesus turned individual encounters into opportunities to touch whole social networks. The Gerasene demoniac begged Jesus to be allowed to join his band of disciples. Instead, Jesus told him to go home and tell his family what God had done. Soon after Levi became a disciple, Jesus and the Twelve were at Levi's house for a great banquet with Levi's friends who were tax collectors and "sinners." When Jesus met Zacchaeus, his ultimate aim was not just to reach Zacchaeus, but to also reach his family and friends. Jesus announced, "Today salvation has come to this house."

Jesus moved from village to village looking for responsive people who would take the good news into the world of their relationships. He built longer-term relationships with his disciples, but he had a harvest model of evangelism. Always on the move, he scattered the seed of the gospel broadly and then watched it multiply through others.

Jesus warned of the power of relationships as a hindrance to faith—a man's enemies are the members of his own household. He warned, "If anyone comes to me and does not hate his father and mother, his wife and children, his brothers and sisters—yes, even his own life—he cannot be my disciple."

He sent out his disciples with the instructions to look for the "person of peace" in each location. Such a person was receptive to the messengers and the message and was well known. The disciples on mission had no relational contacts; the person of peace became the bridge into the community's social networks.

This pattern of reaching households and relationship networks continued in the book of Acts. When the gospel spread to the Gentiles, the entry point was through Cornelius, who gathered his relatives and close friends to hear Peter preach. At Philippi, Lydia and her household believed and were baptized. Later Paul and Silas challenged the Philippian jailer and his whole family to believe and be baptized. In Corinth, Crispus, the synagogue ruler, and his entire household believed. In his letters to the churches, Paul often referred to whole households that had been won to Christ. He described the household of Stephanas as "the first converts in Achaia."[23]

Throughout the New Testament, contagious relationships are the key for the spread of the gospel.

Multiplying organic churches

Neil Cole is a church planter with a difference. In his first year of church planting in Long Beach, California, he and his coworkers started ten new churches. The next year, teams from those new churches started eighteen additional churches; the following year the network planted fifty-two churches. In 2002 this growing network planted 106 new churches. After six years they had planted around 800 churches across the US and in twenty-three nations.

The new churches were small (averaging sixteen people) and simple, because small, simple things are easier to reproduce. Neil Cole's Awakening Chapels and the church networks they have spun off have continued to multiply. There are even great-great-grandparent churches that have spawned five generations of new churches.

Neil explains that these "organic" churches spring up wherever the seed of the gospel is planted.[24] Church happens where life happens. He has churches meeting in coffee houses, businesses, and homes. There are churches that reach out to people in Twelve-Step recovery groups and to the people in local bars. They reach out to homosexuals, occult groups, neighborhood gangs, the homeless, and high school and college students. Neil says that if you saw a hand sticking up out of the sand of a beach and waving for help, you would assume there is a body attached to it that needs air.[25] Likewise, when someone comes to Christ in a new pocket of people, he assumes that this is a "person of peace," and his goal is to find the body of Christ buried in that social network.

When Neil's coworkers go into a new area, he advises them to look for a "person of peace" within a social network. The person of peace is someone who is receptive to the gospel, well connected relationally, and has a reputation—either good or bad. The person of peace becomes a conduit for the passing of the message of the kingdom to an entire community of lost people. The person's reputation gives credence to the message and becomes a magnet for the new church.

Neil calls this phenomenon the "first domino principle" in the New Testament. In the gospels the Samaritan woman at the well did not have a good reputation. Neither did the Gerasene demoniac, but when their lives were turned around, they each became a witness to their community. In Acts, both Lydia and Cornelius had good reputations. Their witness was also effective.

Neil tells the story of Michael who ran a painting business in Long Beach, California. He was a drug addict, and his house was a constant party. The drugs took over his life, and he lost his truck, his business, and his wife. After he gave his life to Christ, God graciously gave him back everything—and more. Now instead of running a party house, he and his wife Carlita host a church in their home. There are about 15-20 people who attend regularly.

After six years this small fellowship had birthed twenty new churches. These believers have sent out church planters across the US and overseas to France, Jordan, Kosovo, and North Africa. Michael and Carlita are always reaching new people and always sending people out to start new churches. They are planting churches around the corner, across the nation, and in faraway places.

Michael has learned to allow the gospel to follow and spread through relational worlds; he has also learned to teach new believers to do the same.

Conclusion

There is no faster or more cost effective way for an idea, a fashion, or a rumor to spread than from person to person and group to group. Technology can never replace the power of face-to-face recruitment by committed participants. Jesus understood the importance of relationships, and so did his followers. It does not take vast amounts of money to fill a nation with the knowledge of the gospel. What it takes is ordinary people, on fire with the love of Christ and empowered by the Holy Spirit, who are willing to tell their families, friends, and casual acquaintances what God has done for them.

4. Rapid mobilization

The best time to plant a tree was 20 years ago.
The second best time is today.

Chinese proverb

Des the Builder

Three years ago, Des Nixon's workers built an extension on our home. A year later I caught up with him over coffee and pancakes. Here's how the conversation went:

"Des, I hear you're building hospitals and factories these days. Are you getting out of building houses?"

"I don't build buildings, Steve."

"Well, what do you do? You're a builder!"

"I build builders."

You could have knocked me over with a house brick. Over the next hour I learned more about growing leaders than I had in my many years of formal training for the ministry.

I discovered Des's mission in life was not to be a builder; it was to grow young men. At our local church he had a ministry of discipling young men. Des was smart enough to know that you don't do that sitting around in someone's living room. So he piled them into his four-wheel-drive vehicle and off they went into the Australian desert for a week.

Some of the young men had troubled backgrounds. Others no longer had fathers around. God worked in these young men's lives, and Des began thinking that he would like to give some of them a job. Previously Des had no intention of growing his business. He was happy working on his own. Today Des has a team of eighteen men working for him. A number of them have come to know Christ through him.

Here's how Des builds builders:

1.   Recruit

Des's first workers came through his ministry to young men in his local church. He spent time with them. He took them away on camping trips. Some came from established and stable church families, others from troubled backgrounds.

As Des developed a reputation for turning boys into men, people sent others to him. Pastors, parents, other builders, and even his own children would recommend young men who were looking for work and for direction. Now Des doesn't need to actively recruit; they come to him.

2.   Select

Before he hires anyone, Des prays and asks God if he should hire this particular young man. If the answer is yes, he employs him for two to three months as a casual laborer. Then Des watches—and his supervisors watch—and the other workers watch. They want to see if this new guy is willing to learn. Does he embrace the company's values of honesty, integrity, fun, and commitment to relationships?

Des has created a culture. Most new workers mature quickly through being in an environment where they are valued and respected and where people have high expectations of each other. After two to three months, the team knows if someone will make it.

3. Grow

Once a worker has proved himself, Des takes him on as an apprentice, and the real learning begins. Des sets standards that are higher than what the government expects. He will even pay to send an apprentice off for two months to work for another carpenter who is skilled in a particular aspect of the trade. Des will continue to pay that apprentice's wages because he wants his apprentice to learn from the best.

After an apprentice has finished his training with Des, he can stay on and work as a qualified carpenter. He then becomes eligible to become a supervisor.

4. Multiply

Des has seven supervisors. He meets with them regularly and shares everything about the business with them. When a difficulty arises, he draws them into the process of resolving it. They experience firsthand how much he values honesty, even when he has to pay a price for it.

Supervisors begin by quoting on and running smaller jobs; as they gain experience, they graduate to larger ones. Des stays in the background and helps his supervisors grow through the challenge.

His goal is that fifty percent of his carpenters will become supervisors and go on to become builders who run their own businesses.

5. Sustain

It doesn't sound like good business sense to turn half your qualified workforce into future competitors—until you ask Des how business is going.

Last financial year his company increased turnover by 43%. His clients are happy, his workers love him, and the business is healthy. Des does not pursue profits; he pursues his mission profitably.

Des's mission is to grow young men. He lives by the conviction that if he fulfills his mission, God will look after his business.

In ten years Des is planning to get out of the building trade and spend the rest of his life in the background, encouraging the men he has grown.

Des Nixon is a movement leader. He knows the principles and practices better than most church leaders I know.

In the previous chapter we saw that no missionary movement can grow exponentially if its expansion is the sole responsibility of paid professionals. Movements spread through the efforts of ordinary people who inspire and equip key leaders. The Baptists and Methodists captured the U.S. frontier by releasing common people to preach the gospel and start new churches.

How the West was won

> *It is hard to imagine any sum of money that would have caused an Anglican Bishop to travel nearly 300,000 miles on horseback as Francis Asbury did, disregarding weather and chronic ill health, "to goad his men and to supervise their work."*[1]

Finke and Stark

When the 26-year-old Methodist pioneer Francis Asbury arrived in the American colonies in 1771, he believed he was called to fulfill a great destiny. He was right—although that destiny was far greater than he ever imagined.[2]

In 1771 there were only 300 American Methodists, led by four ministers. By the time of Asbury's death in 1816, Methodism had 2,000 ministers and over 200,000 members in a well-coordinated movement. By 1830 official membership was almost half a million, and the number of actual attenders was six million. Most of these people had no previous church connection before they became Methodists.[3]

Asbury, like his mentor John Wesley, modeled the commitment required to achieve such success. Throughout his ministry Asbury delivered more than 16,000 sermons. He traveled nearly 300,000 miles on horseback. He remained unmarried so that he could devote himself fully to his mission. He was often ill and had no permanent home. He was paid the salary of an ordinary traveling preacher and was still traveling when he died at 70 years of age.

Asbury's leadership and example inspired an army of circuit riders, many of whom followed his example and remained unmarried. There were no formal vows, but in the early days of the movement the majority of the riders lived by the three rules of the monastic orders—poverty, chastity, and obedience. Methodism was a kind of Protestant missionary order under one leader, adapted to reaching isolated communities in harsh conditions across an entire nation.[4]

Jacob Young was a typical circuit rider.[5] He was 26 years old when he took up the challenge of pioneering a Methodist circuit along the Green River in Kentucky in 1802. Young developed his own strategy to evangelize the region. He would travel five miles, find a settlement, and look for a family who would let him preach in their log cabin to interested friends and neighbors in the area.

Sometimes he found groups already gathered, waiting for a preacher to arrive. He established class meetings run by local leaders to carry on the work in his absence. In one location he discovered a society run by an illiterate African-American slave whose preaching and leadership impressed Young.

Within a year Young had gathered 301 new members and for his efforts received just $30—a cost of ten cents per new member.

Circuit riders like Jacob Young began with limited formal education, but they followed the example of Wesley and Asbury and used their time on horseback for study. They spoke the simple language of the frontier. They faced ridicule, and even violence, with courage and endurance. Above all else they sought conversions.

No matter how many miles Asbury rode, no matter how many sermons he preached, he could never have reached a nation as vast as the United States without rapidly mobilizing these young circuit riders.

In 1776 only 17 percent of the American population was affiliated with any church. By 1850 that number had doubled to 34 percent. Most of the growth was as a result of the gains by the Methodists and Baptists on the frontier. The Protestant mainline denominations (Episcopalians, Presbyterians, and Congregationalists) failed dismally to keep pace with these Baptist and Methodist upstarts. The mainline churches had succumbed to a more settled version of the faith and had lost the zeal for evangelism. Their message had become too vague and too accommodating to have an impact. So the mainline clergy watched from the safety of the larger towns and cities along the Atlantic seaboard while the Baptists and Methodists moved west with the frontier.

The clergy of the mainline churches were drawn from the social elites. They were well educated and refined. Higher education lifted the mainline clergy above the social status of their congregations and turned them into religious professionals. Secularized theological education and social background influenced both the content of their message and how it was delivered. They may have been respectable, but they were far less likely than the Methodists and Baptists to reach the unchurched. Theological refinement resulted in the loss of vitality and movement decline.

They came from different denominations, but it was hard to tell Methodist and Baptist preachers apart on the frontier. They were ordinary folk, with limited education. There was a good chance that the local preacher was a neighbor, friend, or relative. They spoke the language of the people and preached from the heart about the need for salvation from sin. As they preached, the power of God was not only spoken about, it was experienced.

Methodist pioneer Peter Cartwright recalled that, "While I was preaching, the power of God fell on the assembly and there was an awful shaking among the dry bones. Several fell on the floor and cried for mercy . . . ."[6]

In contrast, mainline churches were led by clergy who preferred to educate their hearers rather than convert them. The clergy's carefully drafted scholarly sermons did little to stir hearts. These men were out of touch with the common people, and there weren't enough of them. It was not possible to mobilize enough well-educated, well-paid clergy to respond to the challenge of the rapidly expanding frontier. If expansion had been left to the older denominations, American Christianity may have ended up today looking more like the declining church of Europe.[7]

Higher education and higher salaries made it much more difficult and expensive for the mainline churches to mobilize workers where they were needed most. At least 95 percent of Congregational, Episcopalian, and Presbyterian ministers were college graduates. As a combined group these denominations had trained 6,000 ministers before the first Methodist minister graduated from a seminary. Only 10 percent of the Baptists were college trained.

The Baptists and the Methodists developed strategies that made it easy for gifted and committed laypeople to take up leadership and go where the people and the opportunities were. Deployment was rapid because very little upfront investment of resources and education was required.

Methodist preachers, many of whom were teenagers, were trained on the job as "apprentices" by more experienced workers. They were expected to be continually studying as they traveled. They practiced lifelong learning and graduated the day they died.

The Methodists were centrally governed, and the Baptists believed in local autonomy. In actuality, both movements planted self-governing congregations. The Methodist circuit riders did not have the time to settle down in one place and take control. Their role was to pioneer new works and mobilize local workers to continue the ministry in depth. These self-governing congregations were well suited to multiply rapidly in the frontier culture.

Methodist preachers called the converted to join a growing movement that offered them the opportunity to make a significant contribution—as class leaders, lay preachers, or even circuit riders.

Methodism gave unprecedented freedom to both women and African-Americans to engage in ministry.[8] Women made important contributions to the early development of Methodism. A few of them preached, and many more served as class leaders, unofficial counselors to the circuit riders, network builders, and financial patrons.

African-Americans responded to the Methodist message in large numbers. The Methodists and Baptists were the first to preach in a way African-Americans could understand and, unlike the established churches, they affirmed the place of spiritual experiences and emotion. Large numbers of African-American Methodist preachers emerged following the Revolutionary War. Some were well-known public figures. Harry Hosier, probably born a slave, was an outstanding preacher who traveled with Asbury and other Methodist leaders. Whites, as well as African-Americans, crowded in to hear him preach. Through their preachers, African-Americans played a significant role in shaping the Methodist movement.

Methodist growth was the most dramatic—from 2.5 percent of the church going population in 1776, to 34 percent in 1850. By 1850 the Methodists had 4,000 itinerant preachers, almost 8,000 local preachers, and over one million members.[9] This made them by far the largest religious body in the nation. There was only one national institution that was more extensive—the U.S. government. This achievement would have been impossible without the mobilization of ordinary people—white and black, young and old, men and women—and the removal of artificial barriers to their engagement in significant leadership as class leaders, local workers, and itinerant preachers.

The Baptists and Methodists flourished because they mobilized common people to preach the gospel and plant churches wherever there was a need. The Presbyterians, Episcopalians, and Congregationalists languished because they were controlled by well-paid clergy who were recruited from the social and financial elite.

Unfortunately, the Methodist rise was short lived. By the end of the nineteenth century the Baptists had overtaken them. Before 1840, and during their meteoric rise, the Methodists had virtually no college-educated clergy among their thousands of circuit riders and local preachers.[10] Their relative slump began at the same time that their amateur clergy were replaced by seminary-educated professionals who claimed the authority of the church hierarchy over their congregations.[11]

Adherents per 1000 population for Methodist and Baptist denominational families, 1776-1980.[12]

The spontaneous expansion of the church

The Church was first established and organized with a worldwide mission for a world-wide work. It was a living organism composed of living souls deriving their life from Christ, who was its Head. It was an organism which grew by its own spontaneous activity, the expression of that life which it had in union with Christ, the Saviour.[13]

Roland Allen

Roland Allen was an Anglican missionary to northern China around the turn of the twentieth century. His mission experience and his study of Paul's ministry led him to a radical reassessment of Western missionary theology and practice. He looked for the factors that accompanied the spontaneous expansion of the gospel and wrote about their significance.

Through his study of Acts, Allen saw the church as a living organism that grows spontaneously through its union with Christ. The church's missionary activity does not come from ecclesiastical control but from the spontaneous, individual activity of its members who are led by the Holy Spirit.[14]

According to Allen, spontaneous expansion is *inhibited* under these conditions:

1. When paid foreign professionals are primarily responsible to spread the gospel, causing the gospel to be seen as an alien intrusion.

2. When the church is dependent on foreign funds and leadership. Allen asked, "How can a man propagate a religion which he cannot support and which he cannot expect those whom he addresses to be able to support?"

3. When the spread of the gospel is controlled out of fear of error, and both error and godly zeal are suppressed.

4. When it is believed that the church is to be founded, educated, equipped, and established in the doctrine, ethics, and organization before it is to expand.

5. When emerging leaders are restricted from ministering until they are fully trained and so learn the lesson of inactivity and dependency.

6. When conversion is seen as the result of clever argument rather than the power of Christ.

7. When professional clergy control the ministry and discourage the spontaneous zeal of non-professionals. They may protect the new believers from charlatans like Simon the magician (Acts 8:9-24), but in doing so they also block unconventional leaders like Peter the fisherman.[15]

According to Allen, spontaneous expansion is *enhanced* under these conditions:

1. When new converts immediately tell their story to those who know them.

2. When, from the beginning, evangelism is the work of those within the culture.

3. When true doctrine results from the true experience of the power of Christ rather than mere intellectual instruction. Heresies are not produced by ignorance but by the speculations of learned men.

4. When the church is self-supporting and provides for its own leaders and facilities.

5. When new churches are given the freedom to learn by experience and are supported but not controlled. Allen believed the great things of God are beyond human control. He observed that control produces sterility. Controlled converts may not go astray, but they produce nothing.

Allen knew that a strong indigenous church must not be dependent on outside support and control. He was committed to harnessing the potential of ordinary people and the power of the Holy Spirit for the spread of indigenous church planting movements.

A century later, Allen's views have been confirmed by the vibrancy of Christianity in the "global South"—the developing world of the southern hemisphere. According to historian Philip Jenkins, that vibrancy confounds the myth that Christianity is a European-American religion exported to a passive Third World. Over the past two centuries, European missionaries first kindled Christianity around the world, but "the movement soon turned into an uncontrollable bushfire."[16]

Missionaries have an image in the West as religious imperialists. Yet their remarkable success, according to Jenkins, was not due to the imposition of a foreign faith backed with political and economic power. They succeeded because the church that was planted in fresh soil adapted to local circumstances and took on a life of its own. Leadership roles, especially in the Pentecostal and independent churches, are not restricted to those who have been formally trained in Western-oriented academic institutions. Local leaders are chosen who demonstrate the required spiritual gifts and qualities. Christianity has flourished when it is no longer dependent on foreign leadership, funding, and control.[17]

Jesus and rapid mobilization

When they saw the courage of Peter and John
and realized that they were unschooled,
ordinary men, they were astonished and they
took note that these men had been with Jesus.

Acts 13:4

At the beginning of his ministry, Jesus recruited disciples with the promise that he would teach them how to catch people rather than fish. He refused to entrust himself to the crowds, but he entrusted himself to his disciples. Jesus reached the multitudes, but his purpose was to grow the leaders who would continue his ministry in the power of the Holy Spirit.

Jesus called a select band of followers to leave their work and even their families to be with him. Simon and Andrew left their nets, James and John left their boat and their father Zebedee, and Matthew-Levi left his lucrative position as a tax collector. They became Jesus' constant companions and co-workers in a mobile missionary band.

Fishermen and tax collectors without formal training were excluded from serving in the Temple, they were excluded from membership in the ruling council of the Sanhedrin, and they were excluded from joining the Pharisees.[18] Jesus chose these ordinary men because they wanted to follow him. Jesus invested his life in training them, and he entrusted the movement he founded to them.

What form did the disciples' training take? To teach them about faith, Jesus led them into a dangerous storm. He sent them out on mission trips to teach them to trust God for their needs and to learn how to preach, heal the sick, and cast out demons. They learned how to pray by watching him pray and hearing him teach about prayer. Jesus threw them together in a mobile missionary community and taught them lessons about authority and humility. They watched Jesus' clashes with the Pharisees and learned how to deal with opposition. Jesus' training of the Twelve fused content and context. Jesus' model of training assumed that the disciples did not know something until they had learned to obey it. Jesus' teaching was obedience oriented. He trained the head, the heart, and the hands of his disciples and expected them to pass on what they learned to others.

At the end of their apprenticeship, Jesus told his disciples it was good that he was going away because the Spirit would come to lead them into all truth and empower them to be witnesses to the world.

The gospel and the power of the Holy Spirit were the guarantees of the disciples' authority and effectiveness in mission. The Word and the Spirit enabled the early disciples to confidently release others into the proclamation of the gospel and the planting of new churches. Early Christianity advanced through the efforts of ordinary people. There were "professional" missionaries like the Twelve, Philip, Barnabas, and Paul, but the great bulk of missionary work was carried out by unknown and unnamed "amateurs," both men and women.

In the New Testament there is no distinction between "clergy" and "laity." Every disciple of Christ is ordained for ministry.[19]

Paul, like Jesus, functioned as the leader of a missionary band. He frequently traveled and ministered with others such as Barnabas, John Mark, Silas, Timothy, and Luke. In his letters, he often mentions his fellow workers such as Timothy, Epaphroditus, and Luke. He regularly tells his readers that he is sending a team member to them for a particular purpose.[20]

There are around one hundred names in Acts and the Epistles of different people associated with Paul.[21] He refers to thirty-six of them with terms like "brother," "apostle," "fellow-worker," and "servant." Of these, nine co-workers are in close association with Paul. Some of Paul's letters bear not just his name as the sender, but also the names of some of his team members. Philippians comes from "Paul and Timothy." Galatians comes from Paul and "all the brothers with me." Paul expected the churches he planted to reach their region in depth and to become partners with him in his missionary enterprise through prayer, giving, and releasing workers. He congratulated the Thessalonians that, "The Lord's message rang out from you not only in Macedonia and Achaia—your faith in God has become known everywhere" (1 Thess. 1:8). He thanked the Philippians for their "partnership in the gospel" (Phil. 1:5).

There can be no doubt that Jesus founded a missionary movement that expanded through ordinary people who were trained—head, heart, and hands—in the context of everyday life and ministry. What could it look like if we followed his example today?

Ralph Moore and the Hope Chapel movement

We're not smart. We're just relentless.

Ralph Moore

In the Western world some churches and denominations are planting churches, but very few are multiplying them. That's why Ralph Moore and the Hope Chapel movement caught my attention.[22]

Ralph Moore was twenty-five years old when he planted the first Hope Chapel in Manhattan Beach, California. It was 1972. He had a wife and an infant son. His hair was short, and he wore a three-piece suit at a time when everyone else had long hair and wore jeans. He had no guaranteed income and a car with 154,000 miles on the clock. Like most church planters, he had more faith than sense.

When I spent time with Ralph in 2008, he recalled how that church began with just enough people to fill a Volkswagen Beetle. Soon it grew to twenty, including several bikers, a Marine corporal, a newborn baby, and a topless dancer. By the time the new church had 125 people, it had planted a daughter church.

In 1983 Ralph moved to Hawaii to plant another church. The new church began under a tree in a park by the beach. By 2000, Hope Chapel Kaneohe Bay had grown to 1,600 people and had planted 60 churches.

One of the new Christians in Hawaii was Mel Isara. He became a "MiniChurch" pastor and began multiplying other groups. Mini-Churches are Hope Chapel's primary unit for pastoral care and disciplemaking. Mel caught Ralph's vision for church planting and planted his first church in 2001. Six months into the plant he stood up in front of the congregation and told them he was leaving in two years; he then introduced the man he was training to be their pastor.

Mel's next church plant was in a tough neighborhood. At the first church service, Mel told the congregation he would be the laziest pastor they had ever met because he was going to equip them to do the ministry. He also announced he would be leaving in two and a half years and introduced "Junior" as their future pastor.

Junior was a former alcoholic and drug addict; Mel had been equipping him for the previous four years. Junior had already multiplied five MiniChurches and was ready to become a pastor. In March 2005 Mel Isara fulfilled his promise to hand the church over to Junior and then left to plant a third church in Pearl City, Hawaii.

Ralph Moore believes in "simple church"—it must be simple and it must reproduce. At the heart of Hope Chapel's strategy of reproducing disciples, leaders, and churches is the MiniChurch. Ralph intentionally names his small groups MiniChurches and their leaders "undershepherds." The MiniChurch is where church members are discipled and cared for.

MiniChurches meet weekly to review the Bible teaching from the weekend services. The format is simple and reproducible:

What did you learn? (head)

What did God say to you? (heart)

What will you do? (hands)

The MiniChurch is the building block for the local church; it is also the farm system for future leaders. Faithful group members who are influencing others are recruited as apprentice leaders and trained. Faithful apprentices become MiniChurch pastors. Mini-Church pastors who are effective in multiplying groups and leaders are invited to join a "Pastor Factory." They meet weekly to read and discuss books on leadership and theology. The training is built on the same model of head, heart, and hands.

Ralph believes that the local church should be the "seminary" that trains church planters and pastors. Hope Chapel church planters are not theological seminary graduates, but disciples who can make disciples. Many of them have come to faith through the movement and have grown into leadership in the local church.

Ralph believes growing leaders is like training baseball players. Players need plenty of opportunities to swing the bat; they also need a willingness to learn from their mistakes. MiniChurches give future leaders a chance to swing the bat in a low-risk environment. Ralph has formed a culture of believing in mavericks and of providing challenging environments in which they can grow. Leaders in the making get to swing the bat, and they are given feedback and coaching.

The MiniChurch Pastors Factory provides both theological and practical training for current and future leadership. The cadre of MiniChurch pastors and their apprentices is the talent pool Ralph searches when he is looking for church planters.

MiniChurches are the core of church life. All the future church planters come from a MiniChurch. They start and grow two to three MiniChurches and then take those people with them to plant a church.

Ralph contends that of those who enter traditional theological training, only a small percentage make it through graduation and survive more than two years of pastoral ministry. He believes that theological learning should be integrated with an active engagement in ministry. Education cannot create a leader, it can only augment and improve one. How does Ralph know if someone is a leader? He watches to see if anyone is following them.

Theological education in its current form creates barriers to entry into ministry. Hope Chapel combines learning, ministry assignments, and mentoring, to grow hundreds of leaders; over 90 percent of them have remained in the ministry.

Since 1972 Ralph has seen over 700 churches, small and large, started in North America and the Asia-Pacific region. Many of those churches are now themselves parents, grandparents, great-grand-parents, and even great-great-grandparents of new churches.

If Ralph Moore had planted a church in Hawaii that grew to 10,000 people, he'd be world famous. Instead, he planted a church that multiplies churches that together amount to 70,000 people. Ralph's a great guy, and I hope he lives a long and fruitful life, but if he died tomorrow the movement he has inspired would continue to advance.

Conclusion

Whether it is Des Nixon or Francis Asbury or Ralph Moore—great leaders grow leaders. They reject the arrogant notion that their ministry is primary. Like Jesus, great leaders create opportunities that equip and mobilize others. They focus on the whole person: hands, head, and heart. And they don't just grow leaders, they *multiply* them. They know the harvest is plentiful and the workers are few. They have learned that if the eternal Son of God spent the bulk of his precious time growing leaders, they should do the same.

5. Adaptive methods

In a time of drastic change, it is the learners who
inherit the future. The learned find themselves equipped
to live in a world that no longer exists.[1]

Eric Hoffer

The world's game

In 1974 I finished my final year of high school and immediately
flew out for the western highlands of Papua New Guinea, an island
to the north of Australia. The purpose of the trip was to help build
an airstrip in a remote mountain village whose inhabitants had had
contact with Europeans for less than ten years.

A few days after we arrived in the village an unexpected
incident took place.

The men from over the mountain walked through the night and
arrived early one morning to challenge the men of our village to
a contest. A round object was placed on the ground between the
opposing tribes, and for the next two and a half hours, fifty men
battled to land the ball between two posts sunk into the ground at
each end. They were playing soccer, or as most of the world calls it,
"football." It was wild, chaotic, and fun, but it was still soccer.

At the end of the morning the players broke for a meal of sweet
potatoes and bananas, and they rested briefly before resuming the

game in the afternoon. That evening all the men sat around the fire, eating roast pig and sweet potatoes and singing their way through the night. Before dawn the visitors left for home, singing as they went. Quite an improvement from tribal warfare!

Different forms of soccer have been played for thousands of years in diverse cultures. In the Han Dynasty, the Chinese game was called *cuju*, and it involved kicking a leather ball filled with feathers and hair through an opening into a net fixed onto long bamboo canes. The ancient Greeks and Romans also had their versions of the game.

Various forms of soccer were played in medieval Europe between competing villages. It was a rowdy and often-violent sport as each village's team fought over an inflated pig's stomach. In the nineteenth century the English standardized the rules, and the modern game of soccer was born. In the twentieth century, soccer spread to every part of the globe and became the most popular sport on earth. Three billion people follow their favorite teams, and over 240 million people regularly play the game in 200 countries. There is field soccer, indoor soccer, beach soccer, and "futsal"—soccer adapted for basketball courts.

Today you can play soccer barefoot on dusty pitches in Uzbekistan or before thousands of fans seated in grand stadiums in London and watched by millions more on television.

Nobody planned that soccer would become the world's most popular sport, yet it happened. Why?

You can drop a round ball at the feet of a three-year-old child and she can start playing immediately. Try doing that with American football or Australian Rules football. Soccer is just as hard to master as those other games, but it can be easily understood and played at a basic level by anyone, anywhere, anytime, with any number of participants—men and women, boys and girls, old and young, rich and poor. Soccer is a game that can be infinitely adjusted depending upon the circumstances, resources, and people involved.

That's why it is the world's game.

Adaptive methods are just like soccer. They're simple, easy to learn, fun, contagious, adaptable, transferable, and low cost.

One step at a time

Breakthroughs in the advance of the Christian movement always occur on the fringe and never at the center. So it should be no surprise that the "father" of the evangelical missionary movement was an impoverished village cobbler and part-time Baptist pastor with limited formal education. His name was William Carey (1761-1834).[2]

Carey was compelled by Christ's command to make disciples of all nations. Some churchmen believed that the command to go to the nations was given only to the original apostles and that "the heathen" had already rejected the gospel. Others taught that God in his sovereignty would save the heathen when he was ready without our help.

Carey answered them with a careful survey of the world and of the history of Christian missions. He argued that Christ has a kingdom that is to be proclaimed in its power to the ends of the earth. He argued that it is the duty of all Christians to engage in the proclamation of the gospel. He challenged Protestants to commit to the Great Commission, as equally binding on them as it was on the first apostles.

In 1793 Carey and his family left for India as the first missionaries of the newly formed Baptist Missionary Society.

Carey once described himself as a "plodder" for Christ. One step at a time he pioneered effective strategies that fueled a worldwide missionary movement that changed the course of history. Devoted to India, he never left it.

Carey was a brilliant man. His brilliance is revealed in the simplicity of his mission strategy. He allowed the gospel to do its work through the spoken and written Word in the language of the

people. In thirty years, Carey and his associates made six translations of the whole Bible, twenty-three complete New Testaments,
and Bible portions in ten other languages. Bible translation is hard
and difficult work, but once it is completed, the Scriptures can work
their influence in a new culture. Carey's purpose was to see local
believers coming together to form a church in their culture and to
take responsibility for the spread of the Christian movement.
His simple methods outlived him and became the pattern for the
thousands of cross-cultural missionaries who followed him.

Radically for his day, Carey saw missionary work as a five-
pronged advance. First, the gospel must be preached widely by
every possible method. Second, the preaching should be supported
by the translation and distribution of the Bible in the language of
the people. Third, local churches should be established that were
not under the control of Carey's denomination back in England.
Fourth, workers were to study the background and worldview
of those who were to receive the gospel. Fifth, local believers must
be mobilized quickly to spread the gospel.

More than any other individual, Carey turned the tide of
Protestant thought in favor of world missions. As reports of his
work reached home, others took up the challenge of world missions.
Carey had laid a foundation for the most expansive spread of the
gospel the world has ever seen.

Why adaptive methods are important

> *When you go to war, you need to have both toilet paper
> and bullets at the right place at the right time.*[3]

Tom Peters

Adaptive methods enable a movement to function in ways that suit
its changing environment and its expansion into new fields.
A movement's commitment to both its core ideology *and* to its own
expansion provides the catalyst for continual learning, renewal, and

growth.[4] Dying institutions display the opposite characteristics—willing to sacrifice their unique identity, conservative in setting goals, and unable to face the reality of their mediocre performance.

Management writer Peter Drucker tells the story of a small Indian company that bought the rights to produce a motorized bicycle.[5] It appeared to be an ideal product for India, yet the bicycles never sold.

Then the firm's owner noticed that large orders came in for just the bicycle engines. Curiosity led him to the farmers who were placing the orders. He discovered they were using the engines to drive irrigation pumps that previously were hand operated. His firm became the world's largest maker of small irrigation pumps. His pumps have revolutionized farming throughout Asia.

What made this Indian entrepreneur different? He saw an opportunity when no one else could. He had a small company that was looking for opportunities and willing to take a risk on them. He was curious when unexpected orders came in for engines. He got out into the real world to understand and learn from his unexpected successes. He allowed his customers to become his teachers. When he discovered why the engines were selling, he was flexible enough to rewrite his business plan. When I think of this man, this phrase comes to mind—determined and teachable.

Dynamic missionary movements reject the demand to choose *either* a white-hot faith *or* adaptive methods. They live in the creative tension between them. A key to the success of Pentecostalism has been its ability to bring together supernaturalism and pragmatism in a curiously compatible marriage. The intense religious experiences that give rise to new movements would remain fleeting unless they are embodied in some form of human organization. This presents every new movement with a dilemma—how to give the "charismatic moment" expression in social forms without extinguishing it.[6]

The most effective and sustained movements live in the tension between the chaos and creativity of spiritual enthusiasm and the stability provided by effective strategies and structures. Passion must be matched with discipline for a movement to be sustained. When a movement fails to define itself in organizational forms, we are left with "a loose, ill-defined set of practices and ideas spreading within a population that is never weaned of its traditional commitments."[7] This is a fad, not a movement.

The Welsh Revival of 1904-5 was led by Evan Roberts, whose ministry was based on doing only what the Spirit told him to do. There was no organization and no official leadership. Around 100,000 people made Christian commitments during the revival, and the church worldwide was deeply influenced. Despite this, Christianity in Wales continued to gradually decline. The Welsh Revival was a passing phenomenon that was not sustained by effective strategies and biblical teaching. The spiritual energy unleashed by the revival turned in on itself and was lost or flowed into other movements. In 1906 Roberts suffered a physical and emotional collapse. By the following year Roberts had retired from public ministry to devote the rest of his life to intercessory prayer.[8]

What do adaptive methods look like?

Adaptive methods serve the purposes of a movement without becoming an end in themselves. Here are some examples.

a. Life Transformation Groups

The building blocks of Neil Cole's Awakening Chapels are their "Life Transformation Groups" (LTGs). Two or three people meet weekly to read Scripture, confess their sins, and pray for each other. They also hold each other accountable for obeying what they've learned. The accountability questions are agreed upon, and each group decides which thirty chapters of Scripture to read each week. When the group grows to four, they form two groups. There is no central coordination or supervision of the groups. Groups reproduce all by themselves. Neil Cole believes that if people are reading large quantities of Scripture, confessing their sins, and praying together, it's hard for them to get into much trouble. LTGs are an adaptive method. They are simple, reproducible, flexible, and contagious.

b. The Alpha course

I know of factory workers in China and yuppies in London who are coming to faith through the Alpha course. Alpha courses allow people to explore the basics of the Christian faith in a relaxed and relational setting. The course is being run around the world by thousands of churches representing all major Christian denominations. It's everywhere—152 countries, 21,000 churches, and 80% of the prisons in Britain. Eleven million people of all ages have completed the course so far. The current rate of completion is about a million a year, and it's increasing.[9]

Alpha works because it understands the importance of relational networks. Guests are more likely to come and stay because of a significant relationship. Once they get involved, Alpha becomes a safe place to belong before they believe. They can ask any question and say what they think, and they'll be taken seriously. The shared meals, the discussion, and the retreat all create community around the experience of discovery.

Alpha only works because hundreds of thousands of people whose lives have been changed by Alpha invite their friends and family to participate in future courses. Tens of thousands of ordinary people have been trained to run the courses.

Alpha passes the adaptive method test. It works for its intended purpose. It can take on different forms in different contexts. It can grow and multiply while maintaining quality. It is minimalist: it doesn't need plenty of money, professional staff, or infrastructure to happen.

c. Bible translation

Translating the Bible is not a simple or easy process. Translations can take many years to complete and often must be accompanied by literacy programs. Yet it is still an adaptive method.

Wycliffe Bible Translators' mission is to make "God's Word accessible to all people in the language of their heart." Of the world's 6,912 languages, 2,251 languages do not have any of the Bible translated.[10]

Once translated, the contagious influence of the Scriptures can spread and permeate a culture. The outcome is the spread of the gospel and the planting of an indigenous church. Bible translation combined with education for literacy is one of the most effective adaptive methods in world missions.

The ministry of StoryRunners takes the Bible into oral cultures where literacy levels are low. StoryRunners sends out teams who translate and spread Bible stories orally among an unreached people group in its heart language.[11]

Due to the work of Bible translators, Christianity is by far the most culturally and linguistically diverse religion of all. African-born Yale historian Lamin Sanneh points out that, "Christianity has been the impulse behind the creation of more dictionaries and grammars of the world's languages than any other force in history."[12] He argues that—contrary to popular belief, and in sharp contrast to Islam—Christianity preserves indigenous life and culture because of its emphasis on mother-tongue translation.[13]

How to recognize an adaptive method

Adaptive methods enable a movement to function in ways that suit its changing environment and its expansion into new fields. Movements that drift away from their core beliefs are always at risk, but so are movements that regard the way they currently function as sacred.

Adaptive methods are recognized by their fruit. These methods are functional, responsive, simple, sustainable, and resilient.

Every method must be evaluated against the desired outcome. That means we need to be very clear about our unchanging message and mission and clearly distinguish them from our continually changing methods.

We have a part to play. We are responsible to remain true to the gospel *and* to continually evaluate the fruitfulness and effectiveness of our methods. If we don't, self-preservation will become our mission.

When powerful organizations and movements in one era end up crippled in the next, the cause is often "the failure of success."[14] They become so convinced what they are doing is right that they stop paying attention to the world around them. They stop learning and adapting. Worse still, the informal methods that brought the initial success become formalized in inflexible and complex policies and procedures. Creativity and innovation jump ship or are made to walk the plank.

There is a cure for movements that have lost touch with a changing world. They must revisit their core beliefs and then give the young and the young at heart freedom to pioneer something new. Necessity is the mother of invention. New ideas come from fresh challenges. One of the best ways to renew an existing church is for that church to plant a church and watch what happens.

I sat in a room of about forty church leaders gathered to hear one of the cross-cultural missionaries I work with talk about church planting movements in Asia. He's been in the middle of the action for over a decade. He knows how to mobilize new believers to share their faith and plant churches.

This man told us that one of the key elements of a church planting movement is to ensure that every new believer has a simple way of immediately sharing their story and the gospel with friends and family. The church leaders wanted to dissect his model of evangelism. They wanted to discuss our cultural context. They wanted to go deeper. They wanted to lead this brother into complexity and abstraction where we felt safe. He listened for a while and then asked patiently and repeatedly, "But who could you share the gospel with this week? What are you willing to *do*?"

We were the ones with the theological degrees, the ministry experience, and the resources. He was the one with the new believers and the new churches.

Are our methods so simple that the newest believer is employing them? That's how movements multiply disciples, groups, and communities of faith. They democratize their methods and allow every follower of Jesus to participate.

Methods must be simple enough so they can be reproduced easily, rapidly, and sustainably. Here are some examples of sustainable and unsustainable church planting strategies.

Unsustainable Church Planting Strategies	**Sustainable** Church Planting Strategies
Fully fund every church plant	Train church planters to raise funds or become tentmakers.
Require seminary training for every church planter	Multiply trainers in the field
Provide a coach for every church planter	Equip established church planters to coach the next wave of church planters
Provide long term subsidies for struggling church plants	Allow churches to take responsibility
Parent churches take responsibility for the budgeting and administration of church plants	Empower church plants to set up their own systems
Centrally plan and coordinate where and when churches are to be planted	Expect churches and church planters to seek God, do the research, and multiply churches wherever there is a need
Start a church	Multiply churches
A denomination solely responsible to identify and recruit church planters	Every church planter trains apprentices on their team for future church plants

Unsustainable Church Planting Strategies	Sustainable Church Planting Strategies
Satellite congregations dependent forever on the sending church	Satellite congregations graduate quickly to interdependence and become multiplying hubs
A movement held together by tight organizational systems of control	A movement held together by a common cause and relationships

Centralization and standardization are the enemies of innovation. The truly great companies do not make their best moves by brilliant and complex strategic planning. What they do is "try a lot of stuff and see what works."[15] Remain true to your cause and find different ways to pursue it, then test the fruit and multiply what is effective.

There is only one gospel, and there is only one church, but they must be expressed in an endless diversity of forms. Look around you. God loves diversity. That's why I like churches of all shapes and sizes and styles. That's why I would rather see ten different approaches to reaching African refugees with the gospel than just one.

Adaptive methods ensure that a movement can respond effectively to a changing environment over the long haul.

Jesus and adaptive methods

As the Word made flesh, Jesus fully entered into our world. He chose to communicate and minister in ways that matched his context and were easily picked up by his disciples. His message was profound but simple. It was readily transmitted, shaped, and passed on by his disciples. Here are just a few examples of how Jesus made use of adaptive methods.

1. His teaching

Jesus used unique teaching methods; no other rabbi taught like Jesus. He walked from village to village and taught men and women, large crowds and small groups, in synagogues and in open fields, in small market places and in private houses.[16]

Jesus' sayings and stories were brief, pointed, and pregnant with meaning. They were visual and poetic, and he told them repeatedly so that they would be easily remembered and passed on to others, which is what the disciples did as Jesus sent them out.[17]

By the end of Jesus' ministry, the content of his message was imprinted on the disciples' minds and hearts. These profound but simple sayings and stories were easily transmitted as the missionary movement advanced from person to person, group to group, and culture to culture. His teachings and stories have not lost their appeal or power in two thousand years.

2. Dialogue with individuals

Jesus' encounter with the Samaritan woman (John 4:1-42) shows how he adapted his message to the needs of his audience, even if it was an audience of one.[18]

Jesus was tired, hot, and in need of rest from the journey. Yet he began the conversation with the woman despite the many apparent obstacles between them. She was an uneducated Samaritan woman with a questionable reputation. He was a Jewish man with enemies looking for any excuse to discredit him. Jesus was the bearer of God's revelation, yet he allowed the woman to determine the direction and form of the conversation. Jesus took her background and her responses seriously and used them as opportunities to share the gospel. He used her language in communicating his message. He also addressed her personally and dealt with the key issue in her life. He had a universal message but shaped it in a way that was meaningful to this woman. He was patient and allowed the truth of who he was to gradually dawn on her. She was important to him.

When the disciples returned, Jesus used his conversation

with the woman as an opportunity to teach them how to share the gospel.

3.   Leadership development

Jesus trained his disciples in a way that was reproducible and transferable. He did not place unnecessary restrictions on who could be trained and entrusted with significant ministry. He expected faithfulness to the gospel in word and deed, but there were no artificial academic or institutional requirements for trainees. Furthermore, Jesus knew that the Holy Spirit would come and guide his followers into all truth and empower them for ministry. He did not leave a ministry manual behind with procedures and policies. He expected them to travel light in dependence on the Spirit and, just as Jesus had done, to adapt the unchanging message of the gospel to each circumstance.

Jesus did not come to found a religious organization. He came to found a missionary movement that would spread to the ends of the earth. Right from the beginning, he modeled a commitment to methods that were adaptable, transferable, and readily reproducible. Then, most importantly, he left his followers to do it with the promise of his guiding presence through the Holy Spirit.

The early Christians carried out the mission entrusted to them with great courage, ingenuity, and flexibility. They had no model of an international movement to work from. None had ever existed. There were no precedents. They confronted a dominant, antagonistic religious and political culture with their limited finances and organizational support. Yet the gospel went out through them from Jerusalem to Judea, Samaria, and the ends of the earth. Their strategy was simple: they wanted to win as many people as possible to faith in Jesus Christ and gather them into communities that became mission centers as they eagerly awaited his return.[19]

Following the example of Jesus, Paul took his listeners seriously. He described himself as a free man who became the slave of all for the sake of the gospel. Paul adapted his methods for the sake of winning some. Paul was willing to "be all things to all people," whatever their background. His goal was to win people. But he never said he would become an adulterer to the adulterers or a pagan to the pagans. The gospel—not pragmatism—determined the limits of his flexibility as a missionary. Paul argued for cultural relevance, not cultural relativism (1 Cor. 9:19-23).[20]

Paul was under no illusion that if somehow he could get the form of the message "right" for the culture, then people would believe. He knew that the Jews expected God to reveal himself in power and glory, while the Greeks looked for wisdom. Neither of them could comprehend a God who revealed himself in the Cross (1 Cor. 1:22-25).[21] Despite his willingness to adapt himself to his audience, Paul taught that behind the effectiveness of the gospel is God's powerful presence through the Holy Spirit (1 Thess. 1:5-6).

An important element in Paul's strategy was the establishment of new churches. He did not just win converts, he gathered them into communities of faith. Much of the ministry of Paul and his team was focused on visits and letters to the churches, the training of local leaders, and the correction of dangerous errors in belief and behavior. The churches met in homes and were largely run by local believers. They met for worship, teaching, and mutual support. Paul's aim was to bring each new church to maturity so he could move on to the next destination with the church as a partner in his mission.

Christianity's stubborn intransigence combined with flexibility in methods was a key to its success.[22] Early Christianity refused to compromise its essential beliefs in the struggle with paganism and the social and moral practices of the surrounding cultures. Stubbornness gave Christianity its internal strength, and flexibility enabled Christianity to adjust itself to the social, intellectual, and cultural context. Christianity was adaptable without being syncretic. Syncretism is the attempt to fuse the Christian faith with one or more opposing beliefs. At its heart is the denial of the uniqueness of the gospel. The Jerusalem council (Acts 15) rejected the attempt by some to impose the requirements of the Jewish law on Gentile believers. On another front the early church resisted the attempts by the Roman state and the Greek culture to make Christianity just one of a range of acceptable religions.

Christianity made itself at home in both the Jewish and Greco-Roman worlds and yet did not sacrifice its message to win acceptance.

Learning from "Barney"

I was visiting some of the cross-cultural missionaries I work with in Asia. I was packing to go to the airport when someone mentioned there was a New Zealand couple in the city who had seen over three thousand people come to faith in a church planting movement. After a quick call, I dashed to meet "Barney" on my way to the airport. Barney is short for Barnabas. He is in a restricted access country, and I can't tell you his real name.

The story was true. There had been thousands of people converted and hundreds of churches planted, but in a way that I did not expect. Most of the people had never met Barney. He was known by only a handful of leaders in the movement. In the early years he had brought some of the key leaders to Christ; immediately he concentrated on helping them to win their friends and families and to plant churches. Many factors contributed to this amazing story of gospel advance. The aspect I want to focus on relates to adaptive methods.

Barney began his ministry assuming it was his role to be the evangelist, teacher, and church planter. His early efforts didn't meet with much success, so he decided to become a learner. He looked for the evidence of God's activity in the field. He watched and saw what God was blessing. He even saw God's activity in setbacks.

When Barney visited some communities, the police would arrive to find out why he was there. So he decided for security reasons to play a background role and equip new converts to do the ministry. Soon he discovered that this was not just good for security, it was also good church planting practice. The new believers could do a far better job than he could. A paradigm shift was going on in his understanding of his role and strategy.

Barney became convinced that foreigners don't make the best church planters—local believers do. He discovered he could contribute as a partner with locals through coaching, providing resources, problem solving, and training trainers. He made sure that everything he did was simple, effective, and transferable.

Many cross-cultural missionaries focus on "contextualization." They want to ensure the gospel and the church comes in a form that is relevant to the receptor culture. Barney's first concern is with "indigenization"—ensuring local believers take responsibility for the spread of the gospel. If that happens, they will do the best job of making the forms of the gospel and the church relevant to their culture.

As the leaders matured, Barney became less directly involved. Today he is partnering with them to plant churches in unreached cities.

Barney is also training other local and foreign workers to apply the same principles. He has connected with practitioners in other locations who have been on a similar journey. For each of them these discoveries began when they confronted their lack of progress and asked, "How can we partner with what God is doing?"

In recent years these workers have pooled their learning, and exciting new strategies are bearing fruit around the world. David Garrison's book *Church Planting Movements*[23] captures this new paradigm of missions, which is really an old paradigm rediscovered.

Conclusion

To fulfill their mission the most effective movements are prepared to change everything about themselves except their basic beliefs. Unencumbered by tradition, movements feel free to experiment with new forms of the church and new effective methods of ministry. Movements embody their vision and values in systems that are effective, flexible, and reproducible which outlast and even surpass the influence of first generation of leaders.

Adaptive methods are the scaffolding of a movement, not the building itself. They remind us that the kingdom of heaven must be grounded in every day practicalities. A living organism cannot survive without effective systems that can adapt to different environments. The good news of Jesus Christ is unchanging and eternal, yet its form must continually change in response to each situation. Our methods must serve our message by ensuring that the gospel can spread unhindered across cultural and geographic boundaries.

Conclusion:
The future is already here

With the drawing of this Love and the voice of this Calling
We shall not cease from exploration
And the end of all our exploring
Will be to arrive where we started
And know the place for the first time.

T. S. Elliot, Four Quartets

We have looked at five recurring lessons on what it means for God's people to be a missionary movement. Those lessons are not a program or a formula, and their application differs in every context. So don't be concerned if you're not sure where or how to begin. The best practitioners rarely do.

Here are the stories of two leaders, one in Kenya and one in Australia. These leaders have made an impressive start, and they continue to learn what a missionary movement is all about.

Growing sons and daughters

I visited Africa for the first time in 2008 and met Oscar Muriu, pastor of the Nairobi Chapel in Kenya. When Oscar took over the leadership of the Nairobi Chapel in 1989, he had the advantage of not knowing what he was doing. He was twenty-seven years old and the first African pastor of a dwindling and predominantly white congregation. The church had a dream for the rebirth of Nairobi Chapel as an African congregation reaching out to the surrounding community, which included the University of Nairobi.

Oscar set about reaching university students; from the start, he focused on growing leaders rather than growing the church. He set up an internship program at no cost to the church. The interns raised their own support. Oscar made sure that each intern was presented with challenging opportunities that he hoped would keep them on their knees or at least lying awake at night worrying.

Oscar developed the internship model by asking, "What did Jesus do with the Twelve?" He came up with five things. Jesus spent time teaching them. He put them into teams. He sent them out to do ministry. He demonstrated and taught them how to pray and apply the Scriptures to their lives. Lastly, Jesus prepared them to take responsibility when he left.

By the year 2000, Nairobi Chapel had grown to almost 4,000 adults and children and had planted seven churches. Then Oscar took his commitment to grow leaders one step further. He got his elders to agree that he was only allowed to preach half the time, and the rest of the time he had to train up others to preach. The worship leader led half of the time and trained new worship leaders for the other half. The children's teachers could only teach half the sessions and spent the rest of the time training new teachers. All elders were to mentor the people that would replace them when their second term finished.

Now Oscar had a problem. He looked out over the church and realized he had too many leaders. He knew that if they remained underutilized, they would soon become bored; eventually their frustration would come out as criticism. So Oscar divided his church of 4,000 into five churches. He sent out some of his best interns in their twenties as church planters. He also sent experienced elders, most of whom were in their thirties, to support the church planters. Each church planting team went out with trained and experienced worship leaders, home group leaders, children's workers, and youth workers.

The growing network of churches is now multiplying interns as each new church develops its own program. I visited Oscar in Nairobi and met one of his church planters. This man had walked away from a lucrative legal career because of the impact of the internship program on his life. Over a dinner of barbecued goat I asked him, "How many interns do you have?" "Ten," he replied. Oscar's people have mastered the difference between growth by addition and growth by multiplication.

Today Nairobi Chapel has planted 25 congregations in Nairobi, with thousands of members. Fourteen of the churches are in the slums of Nairobi where the members do evangelism, make disciples, grow leaders, and plant churches right where the people are.

By 2020 Oscar and his team want to plant 300 churches in Kenya, other parts of Africa, Europe, Asia, and America.

I asked Oscar the key to his success. He told me, "All I do is copy. You don't have to be clever to copy. I look at Scripture and ask, 'What did Jesus do?' They call that obedience."

The one statement he made that I will never forget was, "Steve, I don't plant churches. I grow sons." And some of his best "sons" are daughters. About half of his interns are women.

Oscar is a movement leader. He hasn't held onto his power and his position as the pastor of a large church. Instead he has chosen to use his position and power to serve a missionary movement and to grow leaders who do the same. Isn't that what Jesus would do?

Wrestling against flesh and blood

Berkley is a small working-class town south of Sydney, Australia. Unemployment is high since the steel mills closed down. Some families are second and third generation welfare recipients who spend hours every day watching television. Wayne Pickford is a former professional wrestler who had a heart to reach out to these folks. In 2007 he staged a wrestling match to connect with the community—and to launch a church at the same time.

Wayne also gathered a small team who were passionate about Jesus and had a heart for evangelism. Often these people were sidelined in existing churches because they were so zealous. Wayne took these zealots, taught them how to love people, and released them to become the pastors of a neighborhood. They "adopt" one block at a time and begin knocking on doors. They visit every house, every month, with the intention of offering Jesus' love to people.

The team members go out to serve the community and to wait for opportunities to share the gospel. They've been visiting three different people with terminal cancer. Most weeks it's the only visit those folks receive. There aren't enough workers to cover every neighborhood, so people ask, "When will you visit our street?" People are also signing up to join Alpha study groups that explore what it means to be a Christian. Some have volunteered to join an "adopt-a-block" team.

Wayne's qualifications for ministry are his working class background and his experiences as a prison officer and professional wrestler. He has not graduated from seminary, and he is not ordained—but he does know how to share the gospel with people who need Jesus. He does know how to recruit a team of pioneers to go into an unreached town. He does know how to make disciples and gather them together. He does know how to help new disciples reach their friends and family with the good news.

Wayne looks across Australia and sees hundreds of towns and suburbs just like Berkley. He's already thinking about how he could train and release teams to go to those towns. Perhaps his denomination is nervous because Wayne has no formal qualifications. Perhaps existing churches will get upset that Wayne and his teams might come into "their" parish.

If Wayne asked me what to do, I'd ask him, "What did Jesus do? What would it look like for you to continue Jesus' ministry in the power of the Holy Spirit?"

In different contexts, in different parts of the world, Oscar and

Wayne are asking, "What does it look like to obey Jesus and take his command seriously to make disciples?" Their starting point is the gospel of Jesus Christ and the church as a missionary movement. In their own way, they each reveal the characteristics of dynamic movements: white-hot faith, commitment to a cause, contagious relationships, rapid mobilization, and adaptive methods.

News from around the world

Oscar and Wayne are not alone. They are part of the global Christian movement that is changing the world. The evidence of that change is plain to see.

The transformation of Christianity over the last century from a largely European faith to a truly global community has been astonishing. A century ago there were hardly any Christians in Korea. Today South Korea has 16,616 cross-cultural missionaries in 173 countries; only the United States sends out more missionaries. Seoul, the South Korean capital, contains eleven of the world's twelve largest congregations.

It's not just the Koreans; the Indians, Chinese, Brazilians, and Nigerians are heavily involved in reaching their own nations and in pursuing world missions.

The Nigeria-based Redeemed Christian Church of God has congregations in 90 countries around the world, including America. Nigerians lead some of the largest churches in Britain.

India will soon surpass China as the world's most populous nation. In India, you're not a serious player unless you've planted 2,000 churches. I keep meeting movement leaders who have done just that and more. One friend has a goal of 100,000 churches and has made a good start. Another has a vision for a church in every one of India's one million villages and for every one of India's 4,693 people groups.

Every day over 91 percent of the global increase in the number of Christians can be found in Africa, Asia, or Latin America.

Fifty years ago China came under communist rule, thousands of missionaries were forced to leave, and churches were strictly controlled or driven underground. Cut off from Western finances and training, the church in China should have collapsed. Instead it expanded beyond anyone's expectations.

Today no one knows exactly how many Christians there are in China. The estimates can vary from 60-100 million, and the number continues to grow at a rate of 16,500 new believers every day.[1] The vast majority of these believers participate in churches that function as missionary movements with an intense commitment to reach their nation. In addition, there has been a widespread movement within the Chinese church to take the gospel west through predominantly Muslim Central Asia and the Middle East "back to Jerusalem" from where it came. The vision is to send out 100,000 Chinese missionaries, and the sending has already begun.

Over the next thirty years China will continue to be the rising world economic and military power. It will also become the home to millions of new believers and a new center for the global expansion of Christianity.

Europe tells the bleaker story of a secular utopia that never materialized. Gone is a commitment to faith and family. Europe is prosperous, but its society is unsustainable. A society that has turned away from God can only find fulfillment in short-term hedonism. Islam is on the rise, largely through a combination of immigration and the high fertility rates of Muslims already in Europe. The established churches are hopelessly secularized, rendered impotent by the legacy of state support.

The Church of England cannot afford to pay the 1.4 billion British pounds required to maintain its existing buildings. Over the next decade, thousands of these churches will be forced to close.

The news out of Europe is not all bad. Europe's evangelicals, charismatics, and Pentecostals continue to grow both in absolute numbers and in percentage of population. They outnumber Muslims in Europe by a ratio of two-to-one.[2]

As the established churches of Europe collapse, there has been significant growth in immigrant churches among Africans, Asians, and Latin Americans. The growth has been in vitality as well as in numbers. The largest church in Europe is in Kiev, Ukraine. It has 30,000 mostly white members and was founded by a Nigerian, Sunday Adelaja. One hundred churches have been planted throughout the Ukraine. Two hundred churches have been planted in the former Soviet Union, throughout Europe, and in the rest of the world.[3]

In London three of the four largest churches—all with thousands of attenders—are heavily dominated by immigrants.

In the United States a number of church multiplication networks have emerged. Tim Keller planted the Redeemer Presbyterian Church in New York, one of the most secular cities in America. The church has grown to thousands and has become a training center for church planters.

Redeemer has started seventeen churches in New York; it also helped Pentecostals, Southern Baptists, and Lutherans plant another fifty churches in the city. Meanwhile, city-center churches modeled on Redeemer have sprung up in places like Boston, Washington, San Francisco, Berlin, London, and Amsterdam.[4]

In 1996 Mark Driscoll planted Mars Hill Church in Seattle, Washington, a city in which he says there are more dogs than Christians. The church has grown, and Mark's example has inspired others. Mark formed the Acts 29 network and so far, 170 churches have been started in America, Canada, Africa, India, Thailand, and soon Australia.

Down in Texas, Bob Roberts was not content to just plant one church. Under his leadership NorthWood Church has planted fourteen churches within a radius of ten miles. You may be forgiven for thinking that anyone can plant churches in Texas, but North-Wood's church planting arm, Glocalnet, has helped to start over one hundred churches around the world, reaching 30,000 people. Many of these churches are planting churches, making NorthWood a great-great-grandparent. Bob taught me that success is not leading a large church. Success is leading a church that multiplies.[5]

Tim Keller, Bob Roberts, Mark Driscoll, Ralph Moore, and Neil Cole are just a few leaders whose ministries represent a growing trend in America towards a commitment to church multiplication. Church growth, and even church planting, is seen as secondary to church multiplication. These men all share a strong biblical faith, a confidence in the enabling power of the Holy Spirit, and a heart to make disciples in their backyard and around the world.

How the story ends

There are many more stories that could be told from faraway places like Mongolia and Nepal. These are stories of how our brothers and sisters in Christ are displaying white-hot faith, commitment to the cause, contagious relationships, rapid mobilization, and adaptive methods even as you read this book. The gospel of Jesus Christ continues to spread by the grace and power of God. These movements are changing the world.

Do you want to play a part in this great cause?

Imagine yourself in the upper room with the 120 people who gathered at Pentecost. Jesus has commanded you to go and make disciples of the nations. There you are with just 120 people. You do not have the resources, the knowledge, or the power to get the job done.

What would it look like to align your life with Christ's command and to join a missionary movement that will one day reach every tribe, every language, every people, and every nation? To be involved in seeing countless millions make Jesus Christ Lord of their lives?

What needs to change in you? What do you need to do differently? Who will you go on the journey with?

One day innumerable multitudes will stand before the throne of God worshipping the Lamb that was slain. The kingdom of this world will become the kingdom of our Lord and of his Christ, and he will reign forever and ever.

This is how the drama of history will end. What part will you play?

Notes

Patrick

1. Patrick, *Letter to Coroticus,* trans. Ludwig Biehler, (1952). http://www.yale.edu/glc/archive/1166.htm (accessed March 15, 2009).

2. See Philip Freeman, *St. Patrick of Ireland: A Biography* (New York: Simon & Schuster, 2005), xi.

3. Patrick, *Confessions* (Catholic Information Network, 1996). http://www.cin.org/patrick.html (accessed March 15, 2009).

4. Philip Jenkins has written an excellent account of the spread of Christianity in the Middle East, Africa, and Asia. Christianity did spread beyond the borders of the Roman Empire. Yet this was in spite of the lack of missionary zeal within the empire, not because of it. See Philip Jenkins, *The Lost History of Christianity: The Thousand-Year Golden Age of the Church in the Middle East, Africa, and Asia—And How it Died* (New York: HarperOne, 2008).

5. Freeman, *St. Patrick of Ireland,* 75.

6. Thomas Cahill, *How the Irish Saved Civilization: The Untold Story of Ireland's Heroic Role From the Fall of Rome to the Rise of Medieval Europe* (New York: Doubleday, 1995), 128.

7. Kathleen Hughes questions if Patrick's position as missionary bishop was ever officially sanctioned. He begins his letter to Coroticus: "[I] declare myself to be a bishop. Most assuredly I believe that what I am I have received from God." See Kathleen Hughes, *The Church in Early Irish Society* (Ithaca, NY: Cornell University Press, 1966), 34-35.

8. Freeman, *St. Patrick of Ireland,* 141.

9. See Stephen Neill, *A History of Christian Missions,* The Pelican History of the Church (Harmondsworth, U.K.: Penguin Books, 1964), 57.

10. Freeman, *St. Patrick of Ireland,* 82.

11. John T. McNeill, *The Celtic Churches: a History A.D. 200 to 1200* (Chicago: University of Chicago Press, 1974), 70, 80.

12. Richard Fletcher, *The Conversion of Europe: From Paganism to Christianity, 371-1386 A.D* (London: Fontana Press, 1997), 91.

13. See Kenneth Scott Latourette, *A History of Christianity, Vol. I, Beginnings to 1500*, revised ed. Foreword and Supplemental Bibliographies by Ralph D. Winter (New York: Harper and Row, 1975), 102.

14. See McNeill, *The Celtic Churches*, 192, 224.

15. McNeill comments, "Complete freedom from superiors beyond their own communities in the mission field made them adaptable to local needs and opportunities. They rapidly enlisted Frankish and other German youth who, working harmoniously with them, made Christianity indigenous and self-perpetuating." McNeill, *The Celtic Churches*, 175. See also McNeill, 155-56, for autonomy on the mission field.

16. Cahill, *How the Irish Saved Civilization*, 155.

17. Ibid., 194-96. See also John T. McNeill, *The Celtic Churches*, 155; and Kenneth Scott Latourette, *A History of the Expansion of Christianity, Vol. I, The First Five Centuries* (London: Eyre and Spottiswoode, 1938), 38.

Introduction: Why movements matter

1. *Dilaram* is a Farsi/Persian word for *peace*. Floyd tells the story of Dilaram in Floyd McClung, *Living on the Devil's Doorstep: From Kabul to Amsterdam* (Seattle, WA: YWAM Publishing, 1999).

2. See Eckhard J. Schnabel, *Early Christian Mission: Jesus and the Twelve* (Downers Grove: IVP, 2004), 95.

3. See Matthew 12:46-50 and Schnabel, *Jesus and the Twelve*, 355-56.

4. I. Howard Marshall, *New Testament Theology: Many Witnesses, One Gospel* (Downers Grove, Ill: IVP, 2004), 34-37, 709-710.

5. Alan Hirsch, *The Forgotten Ways: Reactivating the Missional Church* (Grand Rapids, MI: Brazos Press, 2007), 82.

6. Following Schnabel, *Jesus and the Twelve*, 11-12.

7. Eckhard J. Schnabel, *Paul the Missionary: Realities, Strategies and Methods* (Downers Grove, IL: IVP Academic, 2008), 29.

8. *Founding charism* is a term used by Catholic religious orders to describe the gift given to a person or group to understand and live out, with intensity, an aspect of the gospel.

9. Kenneth Scott Latourette, *The Great Century in Europe and the United States of America A.D. 1800-A.D. 1914, A History of the Expansion of Christianity, Vol. IV* (London: Eyre and Spottiswoode, 1941), 22, 26.

10. Paul E. Pierson, Historical Development of the Christian Movement: lecture notes (Pasadena, CA: Fuller School of World Mission, 1988).

11. See 1 Corinthians 1:18-2:5 and Eckhard J. Schnabel, *Paul the Missionary*, 356-82.

1. White-hot faith

1. John Wesley quoted in John Pollock, *John Wesley* (London: Hodder and Stoughton, 1989), 106.

2. For the importance of Word, Spirit, and mission held together in synthesis see Stuart Piggin, *Spirit of a Nation: The Story of Australia's Christian Heritage* (Sydney: Strand, 2004), v.

3. Quoted in J. E. Hutton, *A History of the Moravian Church*, 2nd ed. (London: Moravian Publication Office, 1909), 180.

4. Howard A. Snyder, *Signs of the Spirit: How God Reshapes the Church* (Grand Rapids, CO: Academie Books, 1989), 154.

5. Colin A. Grant, "Europe's Moravians: A Pioneer Missionary Church," in *Perspectives on the World Christian Movement: A Reader*, ed. Ralph D. Winter and Steven C. Hawthorne (Pasadena, CA: William Carey Library, 1999), 276.

6. See Arthur James Lewis, *Zinzendorf, the Ecumenical Pioneer: A Study in the Moravian Contribution to Christian Mission and Unity* (Philadelphia: Westminster, 1962), 92.

7. Stephen Neill, *A History of Christian Missions* (Harmondsworth, U.K.: Penguin Books, 1964), 237, and Kenneth Scott Latourette, *A History of the Expansion of Christianity, Vol. 3: Three Centuries of Advance* (London: Eyre and Spottiswoode, 1938), 47-48.

8. Lewis, *Zinzendorf*, 73.

9. Jacques Ellul, *Prayer and Modern Man* (New York: Seabury Press, 1973), 161.

10. Vinson Synan, *The Holiness-Pentecostal Tradition: Charismatic Movements in the Twentieth Century* (Grand Rapids, MI: Eerdmans, 1997), 99.

11. Grant McClung, "Pentecostals: The Sequel," *Christianity Today* 50 (April 2006): 29.

12. Philip Jenkins, *The Next Christendom: The Coming of Global Christianity* (New York: Oxford University Press, 2002), 2.

13. For examples see Elizabeth E. Brusco, *The Reformation of Machismo: Evangelical Conversion and Gender in Columbia* (Austin, TX: University of Texas, 1995) and Donald E. Miller and Tetsunao Yamamori, *Global Pentecostalism: The New Face of Christian Social Engagement* (Berkley, CA: University of California Press, 2007).

14. See Joachim Jeremias, *New Testament Theology: The Proclamation of Jesus, Vol. I* (London: SCM Press, 1971), 64-66.

15. See Schnabel, *Jesus and the Twelve*, 273.

16. Philip Yancey, "God At Large," *Christianity Today* (February 5, 2001). http://www.christianitytoday.com/ct/2001/february5/40.136.html (accessed March 30, 2009).

17. See Jenkins, *The Next Christendom*.

18. Lamin Sanneh, *Whose Religion is Christianity?: The Gospel Beyond the West* (Grand Rapids, CO: Eerdmans, 2003), 14-15.

19. Sources, David B. Barrett, George T. Kurian, and Todd M. Johnson, *World Christian Encyclopedia: A Comparative Survey of Churches and Religions in the Modern World*, 2nd ed., (New York: Oxford University Press, 2001), 13-18 and Sanneh, *Whose Religion is Christianity?* 14-15.

20. Ibid.

21. Jenkins, *The Next Christendom*, 123.

22. Martin Robinson, *Planting Mission-Shaped Churches Today* (Oxford: Monarch Books, 2006), 144.

23. Todd M. Johnson and Sun Young Chung. "Tracking Global Christianity's Statistical Center of Gravity, A.D. 33-A.D. 2100." *International Review of Mission*, 93 (April 2004): 166-181.

2. Commitment to a cause

1. Victor Hugo, *Histoire d'un Crime* (History of a Crime) (written 1852, published 1877). http://en.wikiversity.org/wiki/Victor_Hugo_quote (accessed May 26, 2009).

2. Parker J. Palmer, *Let Your Life Speak: Listening to the Voice of Your Vocation* (San Francisco: Jossey-Bass, 2000), 32.

3. See Dean M. Kelley, *Why Conservative Churches Are Growing: A Study in Sociology of Religion* (San Francisco: HarperCollins, 1972).

4. John Wesley, *The Journal of John Wesley*, January 13, 1738. http://www.ccel.org/ccel/wesley/journal.html (accessed March 24, 2004).

5. Wesley, *Journal*, May 24, 1738.

6. John Wesley, "Minutes of Several Conversations Between Rev. John Wesley, A.M., and the Preachers in Connexion With Him," question 3. http://www.archive.org/stream/minutesofseveral00wesliala/minutesofseveral00w esliala_djvu.txt (accessed March 29, 2009).

7. Quoted in George G. Hunter, *To Spread the Power: Church Growth in the Wesleyan Spirit* (Nashville TN: Abingdon, 1987), 58.

8. Howard A. Snyder, *The Radical Wesley and Patterns for Church Renewal* (Downers Grove IL: IVP, 1980), 54.

9. Wesley, *Journal*, August 2, 1763.

10. Snyder, *The Radical Wesley*, 225.

11. Ibid., 230.

12. See Stephen Tomkins, *John Wesley: A Biography* (Grand Rapids, MI: Eerdmans, 2003).

13. Kelley, *Why Conservative Churches Are Growing*, 119.

14. See Margaret J. Wheatley, *Leadership and the New Science: Learning About Organization From an Orderly Universe* (San Francisco: Berrett-Koehler Publishers, 1992, 1994), 18-19.

15. See Lawrence Cada, Raymond Fitz, Gertrude Foley, Thomas Giardino, and Carol Lichtenberg, *Shaping the Coming Age of Religious Life* (New York: Seabury Press, 1979).

16. See Roger Finke, "Innovative Returns to Tradition: Using Core Teachings as the Foundation for Innovative Accommodation," *Journal for the Scientific Study of Religion* 43:1 (March 2004): 19-34.

17. See Rosabeth Moss Kanter, *Commitment and Community: Communes and Utopias in Sociological Perspective* (Cambridge, Mass.: Harvard University Press, 1972).

18. Jim Collins and Jerry I. Porras, *Built to Last: Successful Habits of Visionary Companies* (London: Century, 1994), 138-9.

19. See Laurence R. Iannaccone, "Why Strict Churches Are Strong," *American Journal of Sociology* 99 (1994): 1180-1211.

20. Rodney Stark, "How New Religions Succeed," in *The Future of New Religious Movements*, ed. David G. Bromley and Phillip E. Hammond (Mercer, GA: Mercer University Press, 1987), 15-16.

21. Christian Smith, *American Evangelicalism: Embattled and Thriving* (Chicago: University Of Chicago Press, 1998), 10.

22. Dietrich Bonhoeffer, *The Cost of Discipleship*, trans. R.H. Fuller (London: SCM, 1959), 79.

23. See I. Howard Marshall, *New Testament Theology: Many Witnesses, One Gospel* (Downers Grove, IL: IVP, 2004), 184-206.

24. See Galatians 1:6-9, 1 Corinthians 10:1-13, 2 Peter 2:1, 1 John 2:18-27.

25. G.K. Chesterton, *Orthodoxy* (London: Fontana, 1908), 31.

26. "Repent, Repent, Anglicans Urged," http://www.theage.com.au/news/national/repent-repent-anglicans-urged/2006/03/31/1143441339520.html (accessed March 15, 2009).

27. Ruth Powell and Kathy Jacka, *Moving Beyond Forty Years of Missing Generations*, NCLS Occasional Paper 10 (NCLS Research, January 2008). http://www.ncls.org.au/default.aspx?sitemapid=6269 (accessed March 15, 2009).

28. Conversation with Colin Marshall, National Director of MTS, November 26, 2005.

3. Contagious relationships

1. C.S. Lewis, *The Four Loves* (New York: Harcourt, Brace and Company, 1960), 114-15.

2. Rodney Stark, *The Rise of Christianity: A Sociologist Reconsiders History* (Princeton, NJ: Princeton University Press, 1996), 3.

3. Origen, "Against Celsus," Ante-Nicene Fathers, http://www.ccel.org/ccel/schaff/anf04.toc.html (accessed March 13, 2009).

4. Stark, *The Rise of Christianity*, 3.

5. See Rodney Stark, *Cities of God: The Real Story of How Christianity Became an Urban Movement and Conquered Rome* (San Francisco: HarperSanFrancisco, 2006).

6. Stark, *The Rise of Christianity*, 208.

7. Rodney Stark, *One True God: Historical Consequences of Monotheism* (Princeton: Princeton University Press, 2001), 51.

8. John Lofland and Rodney Stark, "Becoming a World-Saver: A Theory of Conversion to a Deviant Perspective," *American Sociological Review* 30, (1965): 862-875.

9. See Luther P. Gerlach and Virginia H. Hine, *People, Power, Change: Movements of Social Transformation*, (Indianapolis: Bobbs Merrill, 1970), 97.

10. See Stark, *The Rise of Christianity*, 20-22.

11. Ibid., 20, 193.

12. Stark, *Cities of God*, 3. Following Arthur Darby Nock, *Conversion: The Old and the New in Religion From Alexander the Great to Augustine of Hippo* (Oxford: Claredon Press, 1933), 12.

13. Ibid., 13.

14. See Gerlach and Hine, *People, Power, Change*, 79-97.

15. Ibid., 82.

16. John Lofland and Rodney Stark, "Becoming a World-Saver: A Theory of Conversion to a Deviant Perspective," *American Sociological Review* 30, (1965):862-875. See also David A. Snow, Louis A. Zurcher Jr., and Sheldon Ekland-Olson, "Social Networks and Social Movements: A Microstructural Approach to Differential Recruitment," *American Sociological Review* 45 (October 1980): 787-801.

17. Gerlach and Hine, *People, Power, Change*, 97.

18. Mark Granovetter, *Getting a Job: A Study of Contacts and Careers* (Chicago: University Of Chicago Press, 1995).

19. Malcolm Gladwell, *The Tipping Point: How Little Things Can Make a Big Difference* (London: Abacus, 2000), 51.

20. Rodney Stark, "How New Religions Succeed," in *The Future of New Religious Movements*, ed. David G. Bromley and Phillip E. Hammond (Mercer, GA: Mercer University Press, 1987), 23.

21. Stark, *The Rise of Christianity*, 20.

22. Albert-Laszlo Barabasi, *Linked: How Everything is Connected to Everything Else and What it Means* (New York: Plume, 2003), 30.

23. See Acts 10:24, Acts 16:13-15, 31, Acts 18:18, and 1 Corinthians 16:15.

24. Neil Cole, *Organic Church: Growing Faith Where Life Happens* (San Francisco: Jossey-Bass, 2005), 23.

25. Ibid., 181.

4. Rapid mobilization

1. For this section I have relied on two sources: Roger Finke and Rodney Stark, "How the Upstart Sects Won America 1776-1850," *Journal for the Scientific Study of Religion* 28:1 (March 1989): 27-44; and Roger Finke and Rodney Stark, *The Churching of America, 1776-1990: Winners and Losers in Our Religious Economy* (New Brunswick, NJ: Rutgers University Press, 1992). The quote is from Finke and Stark, "Upstart Sects," 39-40.

2. Frank Baker, *From Wesley to Asbury: Studies in Early American Methodism* (Durham NC: Duke University Press, 1976), 118.

3. See John H. Wigger, *Taking Heaven By Storm: Methodism and the Rise of Popular Christianity in America* (Urbana and Chicago: University of Illinois Press, 1998), 3-4, and Kenneth Scott Latourette, *The Great Century in Europe and the United States of America A.D. 1800-A.D. 1914, A History of the Expansion of Christianity, Vol. IV* (London: Eyre and Spottiswoode, 1941), 190.

4. See Latourette, *The Great Century*, 188.

5. Wigger, *Taking Heaven By Storm*, 21-22.

6. Peter Cartwright quoted in Finke & Stark, "Upstart Sects," 38.

7. Wigger, *Taking Heaven By Storm*, 11.

8. For the role of women and African Americans see Nathan O. Hatch, "The Puzzle of American Methodism," *Church History* 63 (1994): 175-89, and Wigger, *Taking Heaven By Storm*, 123-72.

9. Hatch, "The Puzzle of American Methodism," 178-79.

10. Ibid., 179.

11. Finke and Stark, "Upstart Sects," 42.

12. Finke and Stark, *The Churching of America*, 146.

13. Roland Allen, *The Spontaneous Expansion of the Church: And the Causes That Hinder It* (London: World Dominion Press, 1927), 126.

14. Allen, *The Spontaneous Expansion*, 126. See also Roland Allen, *Missionary Methods: St. Paul's Or Ours?* 4th ed. (London: World Dominion Press, 1912, 1956).

15. Allen wrote, "Spontaneous zeal is alarming to them. When the faith is spread spontaneously both the charlatan and the saint find an opportunity for acquiring influence over others. Side by side with Peter is Simon Magus. In the working of an organization the man who is welcome and at home is the plain, mechanical, orderly man who will keep within the bounds. Not only the swindler but the inspired saint is a difficulty. He appears self-willed, extravagant, eccentric. He is independent and is always on the verge of breaking the orderly methods of the organization." Allen, *The Spontaneous Expansion*, 148.

16. Philip Jenkins, *The Next Christendom: The Coming of Global Christianity* (New York: Oxford University Press, 2002), 53.

17. Ibid., 137.

18. Schnabel comments that, "It is likely that the Twelve had a basic education. They did not come from the rural lower class but the vocational middle class. Pious families ensured their sons received, like Jesus, a good education in reading, writing and memorizing large amounts of scripture." Eckhard J. Schnabel, *Early Christian Mission: Jesus and the Twelve* (Downers Grove: IVP, 2004), 278.

19. See Kung, Hans. *The Church* (Garden City, NY: Image Books, 1967), 493-94.

20. For travel and ministry with others see: Acts 13:2,13; Acts 15:36-40; Acts16:1,6; Acts 18:18. For reference to fellow workers in letters: 2 Cor. 1:1; Phil. 1:1; Phil. 2:19-30; Col. 4:7-14. For sending team members on a mission: 1 Cor. 4:17; 2 Cor. 9:3; Eph. 6:21-22; Phil. 2:19-30; Col. 4:7-9.

21. See E. Earle Ellis, "Paul and His Co-Workers," *New Testament Studies* 17 (1970-71): 437-452.

22. Sources for this section: Conversations with Ralph Moore, and Ralph Moore, *Let Go of the Ring: The Hope Chapel Story* (Honolulu: Straight Street Publishing, 2000) and Ralph Moore, *How to Multiply Your Church: The Most Effective Way to Grow God's Kingdom*, (Ventura, CA: Regal, forthcoming).

5. Adaptive methods

1. Eric Hoffer, *Between the Devil and the Dragon: The Best Essays and Aphorisms of Eric Hoffer* (New York: Harper and Row, 1982), 146.

2. For this section on Carey I am indebted to Stephen Neill, *A History of Christian Missions, The Pelican History of the Church* (Harmondsworth, UK: Penguin Books, 1964), 261-65.

3. Tom Peters, "Rule #3: Leadership is Confusing as Hell," *Fast Company* 44, (February 2001): 124.
   http://www.fastcompany.com/magazine/44/rules.html?page=0%2C1
   (accessed March 15, 2009).

4. Jim Collins and Jerry I. Porras, *Built to Last: Successful Habits of Visionary Companies* (London: Century, 1994), 84.

5. Peter F. Drucker, *Innovation and Entrepreneurship* (New York: HarperCollins, 1993), 192.

6. See Thomas F. O'Dea, "Five Dilemmas of the Institutionalization of Religion," *Journal for the Scientific Study of Religion* 1:1, (October 1961): 32. See also Bryan R. Wilson, *The Social Dimensions of Sectarianism: Sects and New Religious Movements in Contemporary Society*, (Oxford: Clarendon Press, 1990), 211-18.

7. Wilson, *The Social Dimensions of Sectarianism*, 212.

8. See Eifion Evans, *The Welsh Revival of 1904* (Bryntirion, Wales: Evangelical Press of Wales, 1969).

9. http://uk.alpha.org (accessed March 7, 2009).

10. http://www.wycliffe.org (accessed March 15, 2009).

11. See www.storyrunners.com (accessed March 23, 2009).

12. Lamin Sanneh, *Whose Religion is Christianity?: The Gospel Beyond the West* (Grand Rapids, CO: Eerdmans, 2003), 69.

13. See Jonathan J. Bonk, "The Defender of the Good News: Questioning Lamin Sanneh," *Christianity Today*,
    http://www.christianitytoday.com/ct/2003/october/35.112.html
    (accessed April 9, 2009).

14. See David A. Nadler and Mark B. Nadler, "The Success Syndrome: Why Established Market Leaders Usually Stumble—and What You Can Do to Prevent It," *Leader to Leader* 7, (Winter 1998): 43-50.

15. See Jim Collins and Jerry I. Porras, *Built to Last: Successful Habits of Visionary Companies* (London: Century, 1994).

16. See Eckhard J. Schnabel, *Early Christian Mission: Jesus and the Twelve* (Downers Grove: IVP, 2004), 295.

17. See Birger Gerhardsson, *Origins of the Gospel Traditions* (London: SCM, 1979), 67-77.

18. See Schnabel, *Jesus and the Twelve*, 242-47.

19. See Eckhard J. Schnabel, *Early Christian Mission: Paul and the Early Church* (Downers Grove: IVP, 2004), 1546.

20. See Schnabel's comments on 1 Cor. 9:19-23 in *Paul and the Early Church*, 953-60.

21. Ibid., 1337.

22. Kenneth Scott Latourette, *The First Five Centuries, A History of the Expansion of Christianity, Vol. 1* (London: Eyre and Spottiswoode, 1938), 165.

23. See David Garrison, *Church Planting Movements: How God is Redeeming a Lost World* (Midlothian, VA: WIGTake Resources, 2004). See also David Garrison, "Church Planting Movements," http://churchplantingmovements.com/download.php.

Conclusion: The future is already here

1. David B. Barrett, Todd M. Johnson, and Peter F. Crossing, "Missiometrics 2008: Reality Checks for Christian World Communions," *International Bulletin of Missionary Research* 32:1, (January 2008): 28-30.

2. Philip Jenkins, *God's Continent: Christianity, Islam, and Europe's Religious Crisis* (New York:Oxford University Press, 2009) 74-75, following David B. Barrett, George T. Kurian, and Todd M. Johnson, *World Christian Encyclopedia: A Comparative Survey of Churches and Religions in the Modern World*, 2nd ed. (New York: Oxford University Press, 2001), 12-15.

3. Ibid., 87.

4. Michael Luo, "Preaching the Word and Quoting the Voice," *New York Times*, February 26, 2006.

5. See Bob Roberts Jr., *The Multiplying Church: The New Math for Starting New Churches* (Grand Rapids, MI: Zondervan, 2008).

Recommended reading on movements

Biblical/Missiological

Allen, Roland. *Missionary Methods: St. Paul's Or Ours?* 4th ed. London: World Dominion Press, 1912.

Allen, Roland. *The Spontaneous Expansion of the Church: And the Causes That Hinder It.* London: World Dominion Press, 1927.

Spirit, The Holy and Luke. *Luke-Acts.* Antioch and Ephesus: Vellum Press, circa AD 70.

Schnabel, Eckhard J. *Early Christian Mission: Jesus and the Twelve.* Vol. I. Downers Grove, IL: IVP Academic, 2004.

Schnabel, Eckhard J. *Early Christian Mission: Paul and the Early Church.* Vol. II. Downers Grove, IL: IVP Academic, 2004.

Schnabel, Eckhard J. *Paul the Missionary: Realities, Strategies and Methods.* Downers Grove, IL: IVP Academic, 2008.

'T Hooft, W.A. Visser. *The Renewal of the Church: The Dale Lectures.* Delivered at Mansfield College, Oxford, October 1955. London, SCM Press, 1956.

Winter, Ralph, and Steven Hawthorne. *Perspectives on the World Christian Movement: A Reader.* Milton Keynes, UK: Paternoster Press, 2009.

Winter, Ralph D. *The Unfolding Drama of the Christian Movement.* Pasadena, CA: Institute of International Studies, 1979.

Historical

Anderson, Allan. *Spreading Fires: The Missionary Nature of Early Pentecostalism.* Maryknoll, NY: Orbis, 2007.

Cahill, Thomas. *How the Irish Saved Civilization: The Untold Story of Ireland's Heroic Role From the Fall of Rome to the Rise of Medieval Europe.* New York: Doubleday, 1995.

Heitzenrater, Richard P. *Wesley and the People Called Methodists.* Nashville, TN: Abingdon Press, 1994.

Hutton, J. E. *A History of the Moravian Church.* 2nd ed. London: Moravian Publication Office, 1909.

Lewis, Arthur James. *Zinzendorf, the Ecumenical Pioneer: A Study in the Moravian Contribution to Christian Mission and Unity.* Philadelphia: Westminster, 1962.

Pierson, Paul E. *The Dynamics of Christian Mission: History Through a Missiological Perspective.* Pasadena, CA: William Carey International University Press, 2008.

Pollock, John Charles. *A Cambridge Movement.* London: John Murray, 1953.

Snyder, Howard A. *Signs of the Spirit: How God Reshapes the Church.* Grand Rapids, CO: Academie Books, 1989.

Sociological

Finke, Roger. "Innovative Returns to Tradition: Using Core Teachings as the Foundation for Innovative Accomodation." *Journal for the Scientific Study of Religion* 43:1, (2004): 19-34.

Finke, Roger, and Rodney Stark. *The Churching of America, 1776-1990: Winners and Losers in Our Religious Economy.* New Brunswick, NJ: Rutgers University Press, 1992.

Gerlach, Luther P., and Virgina H. Hine. *People, Power, Change: Movements of Social Transformation.* Indianapolis: Bobbs Merrill, 1970.

Kelley, Dean M. *Why Conservative Churches Are Growing: A Study in Sociology of Religion.* San Francisco: HarperCollins, 1972.

Kuhn, Thomas S. *The Structure of Scientific Revolutions.* 2nd ed. Chicago, IL: University of Chicago Press, 1970.

Stark, Rodney. *The Rise of Christianity: A Sociologist Reconsiders History.* Princeton, NJ: Princeton University Press, 1996.

Stark, Rodney. *Cities of God: The Real Story of How Christianity Became an Urban Movement and Conquered Rome.* San Francisco: HarperSanFrancisco, 2006.

Organizational

Adizes, Ichak. *Corporate Lifecycles: How and Why Corporations Grow and Die and What to Do About It.* 4th edition. Englewood Cliffs, NJ: Prentice Hall, 1998.

Adizes, Ichak. *Managing Corporate Lifecycles.* Paramus, NJ: Prentice Hall Press, 1999.

Barabasi, Albert-Laszlo. *Linked: How Everything is Connected to Everything Else and What it Means.* New York: Plume, 2003.

Brafman, Ori, and Rod A. Beckstrom *The Starfish and the Spider: The Unstoppable Power of Leaderless Organizations.* New York: Portfolio, 2006.

Collins, Jim, and Jerry I. Porras. *Built to Last: Successful Habits of Visionary Companies.* London: Century, 1994.

Collins, Jim. *Good to Great: Why Some Companies Make the Leap…and Others Don't.* New York: Harper Collins, 2001.

Collins, Jim. *Good to Great and the Social Sectors: A Monograph to Accompany Good to Great.* London: Random House, 2006.

Godin, Seth. *Tribes: We Need You to Lead Us.* New York: Penguin, 2008.

Contemporary

Cole, Neil. *Organic Church: Growing Faith Where Life Happens.* San Francisco: Jossey-Bass, 2005.

Garrison, David. *Church Planting Movements: How God is Redeeming a Lost World.* Midlothian, VA: WIGTake Resources, 2004.

Gupta, Paul R., and Sherwood G. Lingenfelter. *Breaking Tradition to Accomplish Vision: Training Leaders for a Church-Planting Movement: A Case From India.* Winona Lake, IN: BMH Books, 2006.

Hirsch, Alan. *The Forgotten Ways: Reactivating the Missional Church.* Grand Rapids, MI: Brazos Press, 2007.

Jenkins, Philip. *The Next Christendom: The Coming of Global Christianity.* New York: Oxford University Press, 2002.

Logan, Robert E. *Be Fruitful and Multiply.* Carol Stream, IL: Churchsmart Resources, 2006.

McClung, Floyd. *You See Bones, I See an Army: Changing the Way We Do Church.* Eastbourne, UK: David C. Cook, 2007.

Moore, Ralph. *How to Multiply Your Church: The Most Effective Way to Grow.* Ventura, CA: Regal, forthcoming.

Roberts, Bob, Jr. *The Multiplying Church: The New Math for Starting New Churches.* Grand Rapids, MI: Zondervan, 2008.

Schwarz, Christian A. *Color Your World With Natural Church Development: Experiencing All That God Has Designed You To Be.* Carol Stream, IL: Churchsmart Resources, 2005.

Download the study guide
and stay in touch.

www.movements.net

Breinigsville, PA USA
13 April 2010
235999BV00004B/6/P